LEGAL ANALYSIS

THE FUNDAMENTAL SKILL

LEGAL ANALYSIS

THE FUNDAMENTAL SKILL

David S. Romantz and Kathleen Elliott Vinson

CAROLINA ACADEMIC PRESS

Durham, North Carolina

Library of Congress Cataloging-in-Publication Data
Romantz, David S., 1965–
    Legal analysis : the fundamental skill / David S. Romantz
and Kathleen Elliott Vinson.
        p.   cm.
    Includes index.
    ISBN 0-89089-905-3
    1. Legal research—United States. 2. Law—United States—
Methodology. I. Vinson, Kathleen Elliott, 1969–   . II. Title.
KF240.R63 1998
340'.07'2073—dc21   98-26063
                                                                CIP

Carolina Academic Press
700 Kent Street
Durham, North Carolina 27701
Telephone (919)489-7486
Fax (919) 493-5668
www.cap-press.com

Printed in the United States of America

To our students: past, present, and future.

Contents

Acknowledgments

We are grateful to the following people who read and commented on the various drafts of our manuscript: Linda Charet, Maureen Desilets, Bernadette Feeley, Samantha Moppett, Herbert N. Ramy, Anita Sharma, and Ryan Thomas. Their thoughtful comments and suggestions were invaluable.

We would also like to thank Valerie Epps, Stephen McJohn, Richard Perlmutter, and Donald Polk. We are grateful to the administration, faculty, and staff at Suffolk University Law School, especially our colleagues in the Legal Practice Skills program. Thanks also to everyone at Carolina Academic Press. We are indebted to our students as well as to our own former teachers. Finally, we would like to thank our families for their support and encouragement.

Perspectives

This book explains legal analysis, the fundamental skill required to survive, enjoy, and succeed in law school. The endless stream of cases teachers assign to law students may seem overwhelming, confusing, and tortuous. Law school teachers do, however, have a focused and clear agenda. Most agree that legal analysis is the foundation of law school courses. This book lays all the cards on the table by providing an introduction to legal analysis.

Unfortunately, many students do not see the big picture until it is too late. Students often mistakenly believe that teachers expect them to memorize, then regurgitate the law. Professors, however, expect and demand students to explain the law and apply it to a particular situation. The goal of legal education is to understand and apply the law, not memorize it.

This book explains how to apply the law, rather than mechanically memorizing it or relying too heavily on formulaic analysis. Legal writing courses concentrate on teaching the skill of legal analysis and communicating analysis in writing. Legal writing teachers often use a paradigm or formula as an organizational tool for students to follow when learning legal analysis. For example, the acronym **IRAC** represents an organizational technique often used to organize the analysis of legal issues. While analytical formulas, such as **IRAC**, provide a basic, organizational guide for students, it has drawbacks. Reliance on formula limits the strength of legal analysis. Often, students focus on fitting their analysis into a formula, instead of truly understanding and developing a sophisticated analysis of legal problems. Law students cannot effectively analyze the law, or communicate their analysis, until they fully understand the process of legal analysis.

The purpose of this book is to develop and strengthen analytical skills. Understanding the methodology underlying legal analysis prevents students from engaging in overly mechanical analysis. This book also dispels students' perceptions of the mystery behind legal analysis. Use this book as a supplement to law courses to cultivate an understanding of legal analysis. Each of the seven chapters in this book concisely discuss the important concepts relative to legal analysis.

Chapter 1 of this book contains an overview of the foundations of legal analysis. It examines statutes, common law, precedent, and *stare decisis*. The doctrines discussed in this chapter explain the underlying principles behind most legal arguments.

Chapter 2 discusses rules and how they frame legal analysis. It also introduces the method of rule synthesis and reviews common legal tests that courts have adopted. It explains the function of rules in legal problems.

Chapter 3 explores case-law analysis. It explains how to analyze legal problems using case law. It introduces the concept of analogical reasoning through two strategies: narrow and broad analogies.

Chapter 4 explains statutory analysis. It discusses how to analyze legal problems by interpreting and applying statutes to the facts in a case-at-bar. This chapter also reviews the rules of statutory construction.

Chapter 5 discusses policy. It examines how the law protects the public's interest. Chapter 5 demonstrates the importance of considering the purpose of a law, and how a court's decision might further or frustrate that purpose.

Chapter 6 discusses other considerations important to legal analysis. First, it addresses judicial conservatism. This section points out why courts hesitate to make new law. Chapter 6 also examines fairness implications in legal analysis. It reviews a court's considerations of whether the outcome of cases comports with justice.

Chapter 7 introduces an organizational format called **CREAC** used when drafting legal arguments. The acronym **CREAC** is one of several organizational techniques used to organize the analysis of legal issues. While reliance on a organizational formula has drawbacks, it does provide a useful format for presenting legal analysis. This chapter also provides numerous tips to keep in mind when using an organizational formula in legal arguments.

Each chapter explores the concepts of legal reasoning that lead to a clear, thorough analysis of legal problems. The beginning section of each chapter sets the context by stating the learning objectives of the chapter. Each chapter also provides numerous examples to fully explain and illustrate concepts.[1] In addition, the end of each chapter includes practice exercises to reinforce the material covered in the chapter. These exercises provide students with practical and useful learning tools to ensure a true understanding of the material. They also allow students to apply the concepts to different scenarios. Numerous checklists within chapters summarize critical material. Also, appendices provide samples of legal analysis in various legal documents. Finally, a glossary provides useful and straightforward definitions of terms used throughout this book.

The first time you read this book, read it in its entirety, from beginning to end. Each section builds upon the former. Also, use this book as a reference to review a specific concept. This book is concise, precise, and direct by design. Keeping in mind that law students are pressed for time, this book wastes none of it.

---

1. The text and examples used throughout this book are intended only to illustrate legal analysis, not explain substantive law.

LEGAL ANALYSIS

THE FUNDAMENTAL SKILL

Chapter 1

The Foundations of Legal Analysis

OBJECTIVES

WHEN YOU FINISH READING THIS CHAPTER AND COMPLETE THE
EXERCISES, YOU WILL BE ABLE TO:

- UNDERSTAND THE ROLE OF STATUTES;
- UNDERSTAND THE ROLE OF CASE LAW;
- UNDERSTAND THE COMMON LAW, PRECEDENT, AND STARE
  DECISIS;
- DESCRIBE THE HIERARCHY OF COURT SYSTEMS;
- DEFINE JURISDICTION;
- IDENTIFY DIFFERENT TYPES OF AUTHORITY.

Lawyers, by definition, serve as advocates for their clients. They are hired to represent people, partnerships, corporations, property, estates, and even pets, on a tremendous variety of issues ranging from the mundane to the complex. How do lawyers argue before a court with conviction? Do aggressive attorneys necessarily win more cases? Can lawyers anticipate likely results? The answers to these questions lie in an understanding of the foundations of legal analysis.

This chapter introduces the rules and principles underlying legal analysis. The foundations of legal analysis are the set of rules and principles that attorneys use to analyze the law, devise legal arguments, and predict legal outcomes. Understanding these rules and principles is a crucial step towards becoming an effective advocate.

Few expect attorneys to know the law by rote. The body of jurisprudence is too large and always changing. The rules and principles of legal analysis, however, allow attorneys to fashion persuasive arguments on almost any legal issue. These rules and principles also serve to ensure consistency, enabling attorneys to predict legal results.

This chapter introduces two sources of law: statutes and case law. It also discusses the seminal principles of legal analysis: (i) the common law; (ii) precedent; and (iii) *stare decisis*. In addition, this chapter discusses the structure of court systems, basic principles of jurisdiction, and the weight of legal authority. Together these concepts form the foundation of American jurisprudence. They serve as some of an attorney's most powerful tools. When used with skill and expertise, these principles enable lawyers to analyze the law, make persuasive legal arguments, and predict legal results. The power to predict legal results allows lawyers to anticipate the outcome of their client's case.

A. Statutes

Statutes are one source of law that lawyers use to analyze problems. Typically, students in their first year of law school spend the majority of their time reading and analyzing judicial opinions. As a result, they often fail to recognize the importance of statutes. A statute is an act of a legislature that, among other things, prescribes and governs conduct. It is a formal written enactment of a legislature. Statutes are only one kind of enacted law. Other enacted law includes ordinances and regulations.

Legislatures have the exclusive constitutional authority to enact statutes. The federal legislature, the United States Congress, enacts laws that affect every person or legal entity across the country. In addition, each state also has its own legislature with authority to enact laws that regulate conduct within that state's borders. Congress and the various state legislatures are independent, separate law-making bodies. Most legislatures are bicameral. They consist of two chambers, a Senate and a House of Representatives or Assembly.

The process of enacting a federal statute involves several stages. First, a legislator introduces a bill in her chamber of the legislature. The bill is then referred to a committee, consisting of members from that chamber. The committee reviews the bill and invites experts and other interested parties to testify on the impact of that legislation. After careful consideration, the committee issues a report, including a revised version of the bill. That report also recommends whether the full chamber should endorse the bill. The full chamber then considers, debates, and finally votes on the committee's version of the bill. If the bill passes in the originating chamber, it goes through the same process in the opposite chamber. When both chambers pass an identical bill, the bill is then sent to the President to be signed. If the President does not sign the bill within ten days, it becomes law. If the President vetoes the bill, the bill goes back to the legislature. There, the veto may be overridden by a two-thirds vote in each chamber. Barring a congressional override, the bill could be re-drafted to incorporate the President's objections, or shelved.

Once enacted, each statute becomes an independent source of law. Unlike case law, which courts can overrule or modify, a statute remains largely fixed unless changed or abolished by the legislature or declared unconstitutional by a court. While courts can, and do, interpret the meaning and application of a statute, they cannot amend its language.

B. Case Law

Another source of law is case law. Case law is law derived from the opinions of courts. Case law consists of both the common law and judicial decisions that interpret statutes and other enacted law. Courts have traditionally made law in at least three ways.

First, a court may declare that a general legal doctrine or principle is enforceable within that court's geographic reach. By adopting or creating a legal doctrine, a court creates binding law without any legislative debate or vote. For example, in some jurisdictions, a woman and man who agree to live together as husband and wife, and who hold themselves out to the community as husband and wife, are legally married by means of common-law marriage. This doctrine is a judge-created alternative to civil, or statutory, marriage.

Second, a court also makes law by deciding cases that interpret existing legal doctrines. Law is made with each case decided by the court, because each case has unique facts. When the court applies the law to a new set of facts, a new precedent is created that adds to the growing body of case law. An opinion that incorporates a new fact, or modifies the application of the law to an existing fact, creates new law for the purpose of deciding future cases that include that same, or materially similar, fact.

Suppose a court interpreted a case that required the registration of all motorized vehicles. The court first limited the meaning of "motorized vehicles" to automobiles. In a later decision, the court expanded that definition when it held that motorcycles are also "motorized vehicles" for the purposes of the law. From that point forward, all motorcycle owners were required to register their vehicles with the city. In a subsequent case, the court held that motorized bicycles, or mopeds, were also included. This case also added to that state's case law by expanding the definition of "motorized vehicle."

Third, courts make law by interpreting legislative enactments, such as statutes, ordinances, or constitutions. The court's interpretation determines how courts should apply that law to similar cases in future disputes. Suppose a court interpreted a state statute regarding recycling. The relevant statute states that all newsprint shall be collected and recycled by city residents. The issue before the court was whether magazines are considered newsprint. The court concluded that magazines were not newsprint for the purposes of the statute. In that case, the court added to the body of case law by construing a legislative enactment. That opinion now has the force of law on all similar cases.

1. Common Law, Precedent, and *Stare Decisis*

Courts do not render decisions in a vacuum. Courts, in fact, abide by a unique set of concepts: among them are the common law, precedent, and *stare decisis*. In contrast to legislatively enacted statutory law, the *common law* consists of the rules and legal principles derived from judicial decisions, judgments, and decrees. A *precedent* is a judicial decision or opinion that serves as an example of how a subsequent court can resolve a similar question of law under a similar set of facts. Finally, *stare decisis* is a maxim that requires courts to follow precedent when deciding similar cases.

a. Common Law and Precedent

Generally, the common law is *judge*-made law rendered in the absence of enacted law. The common law consists of judicially created legal doctrines. The "law" is derived from the body of judicial opinions.

A derivative of common law is the notion of *precedent*. While the common law is the comprehensive body of judge-made law, a precedent is a judicial opinion that illustrates the application of legal rules and doctrines to the facts of a specific case. A precedent, if it examines a common-law principle, becomes part of the common law. Thus, a case can be both precedent and part of the common law. Some precedents, however, interpret enacted law, such as statutes, and are not part of the common law.

Generally, a judicial opinion only resolves the facts and issues raised in the action. That same opinion, however, becomes an authoritative source of law for future cases. Courts, when deciding issues, will look to those opinions for guidance. Each new decision, then, follows logically from the existing precedents. Each decision becomes part of the larger body of law and takes on precedential weight as a positive legal rule or doctrine.

b. *The Power of Precedent and* Stare Decisis

The famous Latin maxim, *"stare decisis et quieta non movere,"* translates as "those things which have been so often adjudged ought to rest in peace." *Stare decisis* is the controlling doctrine governing the ability of judges to make law. *Stare decisis* is a principle that requires courts to follow precedent when deciding similar cases. It gives judicial decisions the force of law. These decisions are binding on courts hearing analogous cases. While courts ordinarily adhere to this doctrine, they will only depart from *stare decisis* when absolutely necessary, to avoid an injustice or to reflect current policy concerns. *Stare decisis* promotes continuity, stability, and reliability because it allows lawyers to predict legal outcomes by analyzing prior decisions that resolve the same legal issue on the same or similar facts. If lawyers can find controlling authority, or precedent, they can anticipate legal results.

Stare decisis and precedent are related, but different, concepts. *Stare decisis* requires courts to follow their prior decisions when determining the outcome of like cases. Precedent is the decision itself. Precedent is the substance behind *stare decisis*. Each precedent adds to the corpus of case law.

For example, in *Palsgraf v. Long Island Railroad,* 248 N.Y. 339, 162 N.E. 99 (1928), a railway company's conductor pushed a passenger carrying a package containing fireworks. The conductor did not know the package contained fireworks. The package fell. As a result, the fireworks exploded, causing a shockwave, which knocked down scales located at the other end of the platform. The scales struck the plaintiff, causing injury. The plaintiff sued to recover for her damages. The New York Court of Appeals held that there is no duty, hence no liability, to an unforeseen victim of negligence. The court reasoned that the defendant could not have foreseen injuring the plaintiff, and was, therefore, not liable.

By itself, the *Palsgraf* opinion decided the outcome of one case. The holding is legally binding only on the parties in the lawsuit.

The court's reasoning, however, and the legal rules employed to determine the outcome of that case, are binding on *everyone* within that court's jurisdiction. Under the doctrine of *stare decisis*, *Palsgraf* became a precedent. After *Palsgraf*, New York courts were required to look to that case to decide any lawsuit that raised the same legal issue with the same or similar facts. Why? *Stare decisis et quieta non movere*—once properly decided, a legal issue should not be decided again.

Imagine a system where no such concept existed. If judges decided each case independently from prior cases, litigants would indeed be at the mercy of the court. Every argument would have to be considered in isolation. Judges would have the power to reach conclusions without the aid of a sustainable, predictable body of law. Litigants would have no reliable basis to determine whether a particular act had any culpable consequence. Anarchy? Perhaps. At the very least, without *stare decisis* and precedent, the ability of lawyers to predict a legal result would be nearly impossible. Citizens may not know whether their acts or failures to act would subject them to civil or criminal liability. *Stare decisis* and precedent allow attorneys to anticipate legal results by relying on a relatively stable, and predictable, corpus of judge-made law. Moreover, *stare decisis* ensures fairness because it demands that like cases are decided similarly. The stabilizing impact of the common law, precedent, and *stare decisis* form the foundation of legal analysis.

C. Hierarchy of Courts

The authoritative weight, or value, of a particular precedent depends on which court within the *hierarchy* of courts rendered the opinion. A hierarchy represents the different levels of courts within a jurisdiction. The federal court hierarchy and the court hierarchies of most states consist of three levels: a trial court, an intermediate court of appeals, and a highest court of appeals. A decision rendered by the highest court of appeals within a jurisdiction is binding on all other courts within that same jurisdic-

Structure of the Court Systems

	Federal	State
Highest Court of Appeals	U.S. Supreme Court	State Supreme Court (court of last resort)
Intermediate Court of Appeals	U.S. Court of Appeals	State Intermediate Court of Appeals
Trial Court	U.S. District Courts	State Trial Courts

tion. A decision by an intermediate appellate court can only be binding on a trial court when the highest court of appeals is silent, or has not conclusively decided an issue.

Under our system of federalism, each state and the federal system are independent, autonomous, and sovereign courts, with one important exception—the United States Supreme Court. An opinion of the United States Supreme Court interpreting the United States Constitution is binding on every court in the United States, both federal and state, because it is the highest court in the land. A decision rendered by a state's highest court of appeals, however, is usually the last word on most state issues.

Consider the following scenarios:

- An Arizona trial court is bound by decisions of Arizona's highest court of appeals; Arizona's intermediate court of appeals, when the state's highest court of appeals is silent on an issue; and the United States Supreme Court interpreting the federal constitution.
- The Connecticut trial court is bound by Connecticut's highest court of appeals; the Connecticut intermediate court of appeals, when the state's highest court of appeals is silent; and the United States Supreme Court interpreting the federal constitution.

- A federal trial court is bound by the United States Circuit Court of Appeals for the circuit in which the federal trial court is located, and the United States Supreme Court.

D. Jurisdiction

Stare decisis requires courts to look to previous decisions, or precedents, for authoritative guidance in resolving legal disputes. Not all courts, however, are bound by every authoritative precedent. Jurisdiction is an important limit on the precedential impact of a particular decision.

Jurisdiction is the power of a court to decide cases. Jurisdiction restricts the power of a court to resolve legal issues in two ways. First, jurisdiction limits courts geographically. Second, jurisdiction limits courts by the subject matter they are allowed to consider. Geographic jurisdiction limits the power of a court to a particular territory. These limitations are drawn, for example, along municipal boundaries, county lines, or state borders. Subject matter jurisdiction limits the types of actions a court is authorized to hear. For example, a federal bankruptcy trial court does not have jurisdiction, and, therefore, cannot consider a state criminal action.

Jurisdiction limits the reach of precedent, because it controls which judicial decisions, or precedent, a particular court is obliged to follow. Courts are only bound by authoritative opinions derived from courts that are within the same jurisdiction, as well as opinions derived from the United States Supreme Court. For example, a trial court in Massachusetts is not bound by the controlling opinions of the New York Court of Appeals. A trial court in Massachusetts is bound by the Supreme Judicial Court of Massachusetts, because that trial court is within the jurisdiction of Massachusetts's highest court of appeals.

Courts may, but are not required to, follow precedent of other jurisdictions. Suppose the highest court of appeals in Alaska rendered a decision holding bar owners liable for injuries caused by their drunk patrons. Subsequently, a case with similar facts alleging the same legal issue is heard by a trial court in Tennessee. The highest court of appeals in Tennessee has not decided the issue. The trial court hearing the case in Tennessee must decide the matter and render a decision that will have precedential value for that jurisdiction. Under *stare decisis*, that decision would be binding in Tennessee until a Tennessee appellate court amends, reverses, or overrules the decision. The court could look to the Alaska court's decision for guidance, but Tennessee's court is not bound to follow that court's holding. The court, however, may be persuaded by the logic and reasoning of Alaska's decision and adopt all or part of that court's holding. Alaska's decision, while not binding on Tennessee, may be persuasive.

Consider these other examples. Is the trial court of West Virginia bound by the highest court of appeals of Texas? No, because they are different jurisdictions. Is the highest court of appeals of New Jersey bound by the highest court of appeals of California? No, they are also in different jurisdictions. Is the highest court of appeals of New Hampshire bound by the United States Court of Appeals for the First Circuit, the federal circuit court of appeals that has jurisdiction over the federal trial court of New Hampshire? No, a state court is not bound by a federal court of appeals. Does the United States Supreme Court interpreting the United States Constitution trump all other courts? Yes, because it is the supreme court of the land.

State courts may hear questions of both state law and federal law. A state court may interpret federal law when the litigants raise a federal issue in addition to a state issue. State courts may also decide suits that raise issues of law from other jurisdictions. These determinations are never binding on the other state's judiciary or the federal court, because the deciding court sits in a different jurisdiction.

Federal courts decide cases that raise federal issues. These issues arise under federal statutes, regulations, treaties, and the United States Constitution. A federal district court, the trial court of the federal judiciary, may also resolve state issues when the dispute is between citizens of different states and the amount of the claim exceeds $75,000.

In some situations, a case is brought before the federal bench that raises a state issue, but no precedent exists from that state's courts. Perhaps the case is one of first impression, or has not been conclusively decided by the state court. In these situations, the federal court either stands in the shoes of that state's highest court of appeals and decides the matter by interpreting state law, or *certifies* the issue to the state's highest court of appeals.

Certification, a procedure only allowed by authority of state law, refers a state issue originally brought in federal court to that state's highest court of appeals. While the federal court can use the state court's opinion for guidance in its own determination, it is not bound by that decision. Remember, the state court and federal court are independent systems and are not bound by each other's opinions. The federal decision ultimately reached is binding authority for the federal bench, but is not binding authority for state cases, even if a subsequent state case involves identical facts under the same law. Why? The federal court and state court are independent judiciaries. Federal decisions do not trump decisions of a state's highest court of appeals, with one important exception. State courts are bound by the decisions of the United States Supreme Court interpreting the federal constitution. Analogous federal decisions may have persuasive impact on the state court, but are not binding.

E. Types of Authority

An *authority* refers to a legal source courts and attorneys use to oppose or support a legal proposition. Several different types of authority exist, such as cases, statutes, law reviews, legal encyclopedias, or legal newspapers. Authority can either bind the court, or merely persuade the court. There are two types of legal authority: primary and secondary.

Primary authority is the law. Examples of primary authority include case law, statutes, or constitutions. Everything other than the law is secondary authority. Secondary authority is any source that comments on the law. Law reviews, legal treatises, newspapers, and legal encyclopedias are all secondary authority.

The type of authority determines whether a source must be followed, or whether it merely serves to guide the court. Secondary authority is never binding on a court, it is only persuasive. Remember, it is not the law. Primary authority, however, can be either binding or persuasive.

Primary *binding* authority is any law that a court must follow. Primary binding authority includes any statute, case, constitution, or ordinance in the jurisdiction where that court sits. For example, a California trial court is bound by case law rendered by the highest court of appeals in that state, California statutes, and the California Constitution. Primary authority from other jurisdictions is merely persuasive.

Primary *persuasive* authority is law that is not binding on a court. Primary persuasive authority can include statutes and case law from sister jurisdictions. For example, a California court may look to a Nevada case for guidance, but that decision is not binding on the California court, it is only persuasive.

Persuasive authority includes primary persuasive authority, law that is not binding on a court; and all secondary authority. Not all persuasive authority, however, has equal weight. Some sources are more compelling than others. Primary persuasive authority is generally more persuasive than secondary authority, because primary authority is the law. Even persuasive material derived from the same or similar source can have different persuasive value. For example, an article written by the seminal authority on property law would likely be more convincing to a judge that an article written by a lesser known scholar or student. Keep in mind this simple rule — the more legally authoritative the source, the more persuasive the authority.

Consider the following sources used to support an argument before a state trial court:

• An article from a legal newspaper;
• An article from a prestigious law review;

- A federal appeals court opinion;
- An opinion from the highest court of appeals of another jurisdiction.

Of the sources listed above, an opinion from the highest court of appeals of another state would likely rank as "most persuasive," followed closely by an opinion from the federal appeals court. The other jurisdiction's opinion was rendered by the highest court in that jurisdiction, not an intermediate appellate court. A federal appeals court opinion and an opinion rendered by the highest court of another jurisdiction are more authoritative than the other sources, thus more persuasive, because they are law. Opinions from any court usually outrank authority derived from articles or books merely commenting on the law. The law review ranks third, followed by the legal newspaper. The law review article, a scholarly commentary on the law, is more authoritative than an article merely reporting on the law.

How the court reached its decision is another important consideration when determining the persuasive weight of a legal authority. Was the persuasive opinion a unanimous decision of the court? A split decision? Was a dissenting or concurring opinion included? Is your argument derived from the reasoning in a opinion that bears directly on the relevant issues, or is it derived from the part of the opinion that was not necessary for the decision, called dictum?

Suppose you are researching a legal issue and find three cases from another jurisdiction's highest court of appeals that support your position. One decision consists of an opinion that includes a concurring opinion joined by two justices. The second decision is an unanimous opinion of the court. The third opinion consists of a majority opinion and a dissenting opinion filed by one judge. How would you rank the persuasive weight of these authorities?

The unanimous opinion would likely rank as "most persuasive" because it represents an agreement of the entire bench on the resolution of the issue. The weight of the other two opinions is far less clear. Their persuasive weight depends on the nature of the case decided and the language of the opinions filed. Here, the concurring opinion or dissenting opinion with the most compelling reasoning would likely rank as "more persuasive."

Some measure of experience is required before an attorney is able to accurately identify and weigh the various authorities. Sometimes the differences between authorities is quite subtle. Distinguishing between the persuasive and binding sources, however, is only one part of legal analysis. The difficulty lies in crafting a meaningful way to incorporate the authority into cogent and well-reasoned analysis.

Practice Exercises

Complete the following exercises to reinforce your understanding of this chapter:

1. What are two sources of law in the American legal system?

2. Discuss the purposes behind *stare decisis*.

3. Consider the following questions regarding the court systems:
   a. What are the three levels of courts that exist in the hierarchy of the federal court system?
   b. What are the three levels of courts that exist in the hierarchy of most state court systems?

4. Complete the following questions regarding jurisdiction:
   a. Define jurisdiction.
   b. Why must attorneys consider a court's jurisdiction?

5. Can a court amend or change language in a statute?

6. Explain three ways courts make law.

7. A legislator has proposed a bill that prohibits physician-assisted suicide.
   a. What stages must this bill go through before it can be passed into law?
   b. If you were serving on the committee that is considering this bill, would you support it? Why?

8. You are arguing a matter before a New Mexico trial court. Which of the following cases are binding on that court?
   a. Decision from the highest court of appeals in Texas
   b. Decision from the New Mexico Supreme Court
   c. Decision from the federal circuit court of appeals

9. Identify whether the following sources are primary or secondary authority:
   a. Statute
   b. Case
   c. Legal newspaper article
   d. Legal encyclopedia article

10. You are arguing a case before a North Dakota trial court. Rank the persuasive weight of the following sources:
    a. Law review article written by a law professor
    b. Legal newspaper article
    c. Decision from the highest court of appeals in New Jersey
    d. Dissenting opinion from the highest court of appeals in Indiana

Chapter 2

Rules

OBJECTIVES

WHEN YOU FINISH READING THIS CHAPTER AND COMPLETE THE
EXERCISES, YOU WILL BE ABLE TO:

- RECOGNIZE THAT STATUTES ARE RULES;
- IDENTIFY RULES IN CASES;
- UNDERSTAND HOW RULES FRAME LEGAL ANALYSIS;
- PERFORM RULE SYNTHESIS;
- DESCRIBE A PRONG TEST, A BALANCING TEST, AND A TOTAL-
  ITY OF THE CIRCUMSTANCES TEST.

Rules are important because they provide the framework for
legal analysis. They prescribe how lawyers should structure and
organize their analysis by identifying all the issues within a legal
problem. Rules dictate how lawyers analyze issues.

A rule is a legal principle established by an authoritative body
prohibiting or requiring action or forbearance. Rules include
statutes, constitutions, treaties, ordinances, and regulations.
Rules are also derived from judicial decisions. Together, they
form the body of law in American jurisprudence. Rules, by their
nature, are an important stabilizing force in society because they
allow people to gauge acceptable conduct. They also serve to ensure consistency and predictability, because they compel uniform
compliance.

Both courts and legislatures create rules. Courts create rules
when resolving disputes between parties. These rules can be in

the form of a single legal principle established in one decision, or a legal principle derived from a number of decisions. Court rules evolve with each new decision. Legislatures also create rules by enacting statutes. The language of a statute only evolves if repealed or modified by a legislature. Statutes are rules in and of themselves.

A. Identifying Rules in Case Law

The initial step in legal analysis is to identify what rules apply to a particular legal issue. If issues are governed by statutes or other enacted law, the statute itself is the rule. If issues are not governed by statutes or other enacted law, lawyers must look at case law in order to identify the relevant rules.

A case is a judicial proceeding between parties. An opinion is a written statement by a court that explains how it reached its decision. Generally, a judicial opinion consists of seven component parts: the procedural history of the case, the facts, the issue(s), the

	Components of a Case
Procedural history:	traces the case as it worked its way through the court system
Facts:	the events, circumstances, or objects that relate to the ultimate resolution of the matter
Issue:	the legal question(s) that the court is asked to resolve
Holding:	resolves the question(s) presented to the court
Rules:	principles of law employed or adopted to resolve the issue
Reasoning:	explains how the court reached its decision
Disposition:	the ultimate resolution of the matter

holding of the court, the rules, the court's reasoning, and the disposition of the case.

The *procedural history* of a case traces the treatment of the case as it worked its way through the court system. The *facts* consist of all the legally significant events or things that relate to the ultimate resolution of the matter before the court. The *issue* is the legal question(s) that the court is asked to resolve. The *holding* answers the question(s) presented to the court. The *rules* are the principles of law employed or adopted to resolve the issue. The *reasoning* explains how the court reached its decision. Finally, the *disposition* is the ultimate settlement of the matter.

Some opinions clearly express the relevant rules. In others courts implicitly apply rules without expressly articulating them. In these situations, students must learn to extract the rules from the decision. Identifying implicit rules requires two steps. First, identify the reasoning of the opinion. Second, redact all the specific facts from that reasoning. The remaining language is the rule, a principle of law. Consider the following formula:

Reasoning – Specific facts = A Rule

Suppose a court was asked to consider whether a contract was enforceable. The buyer orally promised to pay $675 for the seller's stereo. The court held that the contract for the sale-of-goods was unenforceable. The court reasoned that an oral contract for the sale of a stereo which exceeds $499 is unenforceable, because the buyer did not sign a written agreement, which raised an inference of fraud.

To determine the rule, remove the specific facts of the case from the reasoning of the court. The specific facts, such as a sale of a stereo for $675, can be redacted. Employing the formula, the rule could be "contracts for the sale of goods in excess of $499 must be in writing and signed by the buyer."

B. Rule Synthesis

In some instances, courts state a holding that is specific to facts of the case before it, but neglect to expressly articulate a specific rule. In other instances, courts state a rule, but not clearly. Still other courts articulate a piece of a rule, and other opinions are needed to complete the legal thought. Rule synthesis is a process that formulates a complete rule from its component parts. Using rule synthesis, attorneys draft a rule of law that incorporates the holdings in several cases.

If, after researching a particular area of law, you discover that there is no clearly articulated rule that addresses the entire issue, synthesize a rule. Carefully read other applicable cases, and identify the holdings and any rules articulated. Look for a relevant thread between the different cases. Then blend relevant cases to develop a holistic rule that incorporates all the holdings of the applicable authority.

For example, you discover the following cases decided by the highest court of appeals in your state:

Case 1: The Defendant spray-painted an obscene message on a public sidewalk. He intended to offend passing pedestrians. Held: Defendant is guilty of malicious mischief.

Case 2: The Defendant accidentally destroyed his neighbor's rosebush. Held: Defendant is not guilty of malicious mischief.

Case 3: The Defendant intentionally ran over his mother-in-law's lawn statute, breaking it into thousands of pieces. Held: Defendant is guilty of malicious mischief.

Case 4: The Defendant threw a rock at his neighbor's window. It missed. Held: Defendant is not guilty of malicious mischief.

Case 5: The Defendant intentionally destroyed his friend's bicycle. Held: Defendant is guilty of malicious mischief.

Case 6: The Defendant thought she destroyed her boyfriend's stereo, but it actually belonged to her. Held: Defendant is not guilty of malicious mischief.

Synthesize the holdings of these six compatible cases and draft a rule of law that defines the crime of malicious mischief. Pull out the rule from each case by determining the fact-neutral legal principle derived from that case. A rule for Cases 1 and 2 might state: A defendant must intend the act. A rule for Cases 3 and 4 might state: A defendant must damage or destroy property. A rule for Cases 5 and 6 might state: A defendant must damage or destroy the property of another.

Combine each component to develop a holistic rule that incorporates all the holdings of the applicable authority. The rule that results from synthesizing these cases might state: In order to establish a case for malicious mischief, a defendant must intend to damage or destroy the property of another.

Rule synthesis combines parts of a rule into one legal principle that merges all the components. Rule synthesis also serves as an organizational tool when analyzing an issue. Each part of a rule becomes a separate point of analysis, organized around the general rule.

For example, the analysis of malicious mischief would likely contain three parts. Each part would discuss one element of malicious mischief derived from the case law. As such, the argument would likely analyze: (1) the defendant's intent; (2) to destroy or damage; (3) another's property. Bear in mind, your research may reveal further issues, such as defenses to malicious mischief, which should also be included in the analysis.

C. Tests

Some legal problems require the application of a legal test. A test is an inquiry that determines whether a rule has been satisfied. Tests may consist of parts, such as elements, factors, or prongs. Elements are requirements that must be satisfied to meet a test. Factors, in contrast, are considerations that guide the court. Every factor need not weigh in favor of your client, so long as some factors do weigh in favor of your client. Prongs may be either elements or factors. There are several different types of tests, including: the prong test, the balancing test, and the totality test.

1. Prong Test

One type of test, the prong test, is an inquiry that requires consideration of several parts in order to satisfy a rule. Courts sometimes refer to these parts as prongs. Prongs can be considered either elements or factors. Prongs are the sub-parts that make up a test.

Like the various parts of a synthesized rule, prong tests also help shape the structure of the analysis. Each prong represents an issue that lawyers analyze. If prongs are elements, lawyers must determine if each is satisfied. If prongs are factors, lawyers must determine how the court will weigh each one.

The following example of a two-pronged test illustrates how prong tests frame legal analysis: Police must submit an affidavit to a court before they can secure a search warrant. That affidavit must show that the police have probable cause to search a defendant's property for contraband. Sometimes that affidavit is based on information obtained from a police informant. Under these circumstances, an affidavit must satisfy a prong test in order for an informant's information to provide probable cause for a police search. This test has two prongs: (1) the "basis of knowledge prong"; some underlying occurrences that led the informant to conclude that contraband was where the informant claimed it was located, and (2) the "veracity prong"; some underlying event that led the police to conclude that the informant was credible or reliable.

Suppose you are asked to consider whether an affidavit for a search warrant is supported by probable cause. The above two-prong test shapes the structure of your analysis. The test reveals two elements: the basis of knowledge prong and the veracity prong. Thus, the analysis should have two component parts. First, consider whether the facts in your case satisfy the first prong: the basis of knowledge. Next, consider whether the facts in your case satisfy the second prong: veracity. Whenever a prong test applies to a legal issue, the analysis is framed by examining each prong within the test.

2. Balancing Test

A balancing test is another type of legal inquiry. A balancing test consists of several factors that courts carefully weigh in order to reach a conclusion. In a balancing test, courts balance several considerations, looking at the quality or strength of the argument for each.

A balancing test weighs competing factors. A factor is different from an element. Unlike elements which must be satisfied, factors are weighed. Courts do not use a quantitative checklist that is required when tests consist of elements. The key word to consider is "balance." If one factor strongly weighs in favor of one party, even if other factors weigh in favor of the opposing party, then the former party may still prevail. A party does not need to prevail on every consideration to prevail overall. Courts do not weigh only the quantity of factors that support one party. Courts also weigh the strength of the argument that support each factor balanced. Like a prong test, the balancing test also frames the analysis, because each factor must be separately analyzed.

The following example will illustrate how a balancing test frames legal analysis. The United States Supreme Court articulated a balancing test for courts to apply when a defendant claims a violation of the right to a speedy trial under the Sixth Amendment. The Court balances four factors: (1) length of the delay, (2) reason for the delay, (3) defendants' assertion of their right to a speedy trial, and (4) prejudice that defendants suffer due to the delay. The court must weigh all of these factors to determine the outcome of a case.

This balancing test outlines the framework of the analysis, because the test is organized around each of the four factors. The analysis should focus on how the court weighs each factor. The analysis should also concentrate on how the court weighs all the factors collectively in order to determine the ultimate outcome of the case.

3. Totality of the Circumstances Test

A totality of the circumstances test is another legal inquiry that courts use to determine the outcome of issues. Unlike a balancing test that has a set number of considerations, a totality of the circumstances test requires the court to consider all of the circumstances of a case. The analysis, then, should examine all the relevant circumstances, and not any particular one. Unlike the balancing test and the prong test, which provide a specific framework for the analysis, the totality of the circumstances test loosely frames the analysis by indicating the broad scope of the court's consideration.

Consider the following totality of the circumstances test: A law states that defendants' confessions are admissible only if they are voluntary, and not coerced. To determine whether a defendant's confession is voluntary, courts apply a totality of the circumstances test. The court considers the totality of all the circumstances surrounding the confession, not merely one isolated component. For instance, the court may consider circumstances regarding the confession, such as the mental state of the defendant when he confessed, the demeanor of the officers, and whether the defendant was denied food, sleep, or counsel. The

court will not consider anything outside the totality of circumstances surrounding the confession, such as the alleged crime
committed. Thus, the analysis is broadly framed by including all
the circumstances surrounding the confession.

The tests discussed in this chapter are not an exhaustive list.
Rather, they illustrate some of the common tests lawyers and
courts use when analyzing legal issues. The importance of all tests
is that they provide a framework for legal analysis.

Practice Exercises

Complete the following exercises to reinforce your understanding of this chapter.

1. How do attorneys identify rules in cases?

2. How does a rule frame legal analysis?

3. Complete the following questions:
   a. Name three types of tests.
   b. Explain the tests you have identified in part (a).

4. What is the difference between an element and a factor?

5. Identify the rule in the following opinion.

   Naomi owned several acres of land. She prided herself on her beautiful gardens. Periodically, intruders would enter her property and ruin her gardens. Naomi decided to take action in order to protect her property. She built an electrified fence around her land. One night, Ariel attempted to enter Naomi's land. He tried to climb over the electric fence and suffered a severe electric shock. Ariel was hospitalized for his injuries and may die. He is now suing Naomi for battery. This court must decide whether Naomi has a defense to the battery claim.

   Held: Naomi is liable for battery. Naomi did not use reasonable force in this case to protect her property. Ariel's invasion of property did not threaten harm to any person, yet Naomi used excessive force causing serious bodily harm or death. Naomi's use of force to defend her property was inappropriate.

6. Identify the rule of law in the following opinion.

   On his sixteenth birthday, John agreed to sell his bicycle to Ms. Lupo for $100. Two weeks later, John decided to keep his bicycle, and would not sell it to Ms. Lupo. Ms. Lupo sued. We hold that John did not breach the contract. Children eighteen years or younger cannot be held responsible for any contract they enter into. They are too young to appreciate the magnitude of a contractual promise.

7. Synthesize a rule for trespass from the following cases.

   Case 1: Defendant entered plaintiff's land. Defendant did not know plaintiff owned the land. Held: Defendant is liable for trespass.

   Case 2: Defendant was pushed onto plaintiff's land. Held: Defendant is not liable for trespass.

   Case 3: Plaintiff invited defendant to enter her land. Held: Defendant is not liable for trespass.

8. Synthesize a rule for the crime of conspiracy from the following cases:

   Case 1: The Defendant and Todd agreed to commit a crime on the following evening. Held: Defendant entered into a conspiracy.

   Case 2: The Defendant agreed to help Shelly commit a crime on the following evening, but the Defendant thought Shelly was joking. Held: Defendant did not enter into a conspiracy.

   Case 3: Daniel agreed to help Paul commit a crime on the following evening. Paul was an undercover police officer who never intended to complete the crime. Held: Paul did not enter into a conspiracy.

9. Suppose a law exists that requires courts to consider several factors when determining the amount and duration of alimony. These factors include:

   - the standard of living of the parties during the marriage;
   - earning potential of the spouses;
   - contributions of spouses during marriage;
   - length of marriage;
   - income and assets of each spouse; and
   - age and health of spouses.

You represent a client in a divorce action who is seeking alimony from her husband. A number of months before the divorce action, she discovered her husband's infidelity. She and her husband have been married for twenty years. Your client is 55 years old. Her husband is 53 years old and a college-educated accountant. Your client was a home-maker and never worked outside the home. The couple enjoyed a middle-class lifestyle. Your client has a high-school education. You seek to persuade the court to award your client alimony.

Using the law articulated above, how would an attorney organize and frame an analysis of whether a court will award her client alimony?

10. Your client has a fatal disease that is highly contagious and was warned about the different ways this disease can be transmitted. One way the disease could be transmitted is when bodily fluids of the infected person mix with bodily fluids of another. The more your client struggled with his illness, the more bitter he became. He felt that he was a good person and it was unfair that he should be struck with a fatal disease. He vowed that he would not die quietly and that somehow he would get revenge. One day, your client was walking down the street. A man pushed your client aside and continued walking. Your client became angry and confronted the man. They began to fight. Your client bit the man's hand. As a result, your client transmitted his fatal disease to the man. The man subsequently died.

Your client has been charged with murder. Murder is defined as the unlawful killing of a person with malice aforethought. Malice aforethought can be shown by any one of three prongs: 1) specific intent to kill, 2) specific intent to cause grievous bodily injury, or 3) in circumstances known to defendant, would a reasonable person know of a substantial likelihood that death would result. Explain how the prong test will frame your analysis of your client's case.

11. The test used to establish undue influence consists of three elements: 1) the existence of influence, 2) the exertion of influence that resulted in corrupting the mind of the deceased, and 3) that the provisions at issue in a will would not have been drafted, but for the influence. The plaintiff's brother inherited the bulk of their mother's estate through her will. The plaintiff claims her brother unduly influenced their mother.

How will the test for undue influence frame your analysis of this legal problem?

Chapter 3

Case-Law Analysis

Objectives

WHEN YOU FINISH READING THIS CHAPTER AND COMPLETE THE
EXERCISES, YOU WILL BE ABLE TO:

- UNDERSTAND ANALOGICAL ANALYSIS;
- DEFINE AND IDENTIFY CRITICAL FACTS;
- PERFORM CASE SYNTHESIS;
- EXTRAPOLATE CRITICAL FACTS;
- DEVISE NARROW ANALOGIES;
- DEVISE BROAD ANALOGIES.

The unique way lawyers look at legal problems has developed
over many years in many courts. While seemingly combative and
argumentative, legal argument requires careful analysis of the
legal issues and the controlling authority. Measured reason, cre-
ativity, and dispassionate logic are far more important than court-
room drama or a "smoking gun." There is no single method of
legal analysis. Instead, many different strategies are employed.

This chapter focuses on case-law analysis. Case-law analysis is
one type of legal analysis that employs analogical reasoning. Two
analogical strategies will be discussed: the narrow analogy and the
broad analogy. Narrow analogies focus on direct fact comparisons
between the precedent and the case-at-bar. Broad analogies focus
on the significance of the material facts in the precedents and the
case-at-bar, and how they relate to the court's reasoning. The nature of the action, the complexity of the issues involved, and the

facts all help determine which strategy would most likely prevail for a particular lawsuit.

After identifying the legal issues involved in a particular case, lawyers research for law that applies to those issues. That research could uncover legal treatises, articles, authoritative text, and, most importantly, case law and statutes. Lawyers research for primarily two reasons. First, they research to better understand a particular area of law that speaks to the issues raised in their case. Second, they research to discover binding and persuasive authority, including cases. Lawyers use this authoritative case law to support their arguments and win cases.

Lawyers carefully scrutinize the body of law applicable to their issue to discern the legal reasoning behind the court's holding, and to identify the key, or critical, facts of the case. If the reasoning of the precedent is applicable to the case-at-bar, and the precedent addresses the same issues, then an attorney will compare the precedent to the case-at-bar. If the facts and the reasoning of the controlling authority have a meaningful and significant relationship to the facts of your case, either because the facts are parallel, or share common characteristics, then analogical reasoning is appropriate.

A. Analogical Analysis

Analogical analysis focuses on analogies. An analogy is an inference that if two or more facts or characteristics are similar in one respect, they will be similar in other respects. Narrow analogies infer that a fact found in the case-at-bar is directly similar to a fact found in the precedent. Broad analogies infer that a characteristic of a fact found in the case-at-bar is similar to a characteristic of a fact found in precedent.

Analogical analysis is grounded in the fundamental principles discussed in Chapter 1. Chapter 1 explored precedent and *stare decisis*. Under *stare decisis*, a court must look to precedent when deciding cases before it. A legal analogy contends that if key facts found in the precedent and your case are similar, and the legal issues addressed are the same, then the court should rule similarly in both cases. In cases where the facts are not readily comparable, an analogy contends that if some characteristic of key facts found in the precedent and your case are similar, and the issues addressed are the same, then the court should rule similarly in both cases.

Bear in mind that a precedent can be a double-edged sword. Both a plaintiff and a defendant can use the same case, employ an analogy, and reach dramatically different conclusions. If the precedent's holding is favorable to a lawyer's legal position, then a lawyer will draw an analogy between the precedent and the case-at-bar. Conversely, if the holding is damaging to the lawyer's position, then that lawyer will draw a distinction. Both sides try to persuade the court that their position is more persuasive, and better supported by the case law. The lawyer who presents the more clear, precise, and significant comparison should prevail.

Consider the following example: In order to constitute common-law battery, a defendant must unlawfully touch a plaintiff. Suppose the senior partner of your firm asked you to determine whether the defendant committed a battery against your client when the defendant hit your client with his umbrella, causing injury. After a careful review of the applicable case law in your jurisdiction, you discover one case that is "on-point," or dispositive of your legal issue, the *Cane* case. In that case, the court ruled in favor of the plaintiff, and held that when the defendant hit the plaintiff with a cane, she "touched" that plaintiff for the purposes of common-law battery. The *Cane* court reasoned that the defendant was liable even though the defendant never touched the plaintiff with her person, but rather with an instrumentality that was within the control of the defendant.

The *Cane* case is relevant because that court considered the issue of common-law battery, the same issue raised in your case. The court held in favor of the plaintiff, a result you want. In addition, the reasoning of the *Cane* opinion is applicable to your facts. That court reasoned that a cane was an instrumentality within the control of the defendant. In that case, the cane satisfied the touching requirement of common-law battery, despite the fact that the defendant never touched the plaintiff with his person. Your case also involves an instrumentality, and not a direct touching, so the *Cane* reasoning is applicable to your case.

Also, the facts of your case lend themselves to a reasonable fact analogy. An analogy is appropriate in this scenario because the reasoning of the precedent is applicable to your issue, and the facts are readily comparable. A cane and an umbrella share meaningful and significant attributes. Both objects are an extension of the bearer's arm and within his direct control. If you can persuade the court that the reasoning of *Cane* is applicable to your case, and the facts in the *Cane* case are similar to the facts in your case, then under *stare decisis,* that court should also rule in your favor because the two cases are legally analogous.

Analogies are appropriate when the facts of the precedent, or the significance of those facts, are comparable to the case-at-bar. Lawyers make this determination on a case-by-case basis. Successful analogies, however, depend on two fundamental skills: (1) accurately identifying the *critical facts* of the controlling authority and the case-at-bar; and (2) accurately *synthesizing* cases.

1. Critical Facts

Critical facts are facts from the controlling precedent that the court found dispositive when it resolved a legal dispute. Generally, most trials resolve fact disputes, and courts apply the law only to the particular facts before it. A dispute is resolved when the court rules that, under the law, a particular result is required. Students must carefully read cases to clearly identify facts that the court used to reach a final determination of the matter. Those determinative facts, or some characteristic of those facts, can be used to draw a legal analogy or distinction between the precedent and your case.

To identify critical facts, examine the reasoning of the precedent. The reasoning explains the legal basis of the court's decision. In many instances, you cannot identify the key facts without first understanding how the facts relate to the reasoning of the case. The reasoning of the case determines which facts are significant or dispositive. Some facts in the precedent, although seemingly comparable to the facts in the case-at-bar, may not be critical facts if they are not relevant to the court's reasoning.

Consider the following random facts:

Daughter   *Mother*   *Aunt*

Suppose a court considered whether the words *daughter* and *mother* belonged in the same category. The court held that they both belonged in the same category. What was the court's reasoning? Was the reasoning based on the number of syllables in a word, based on words that represent the same gender, or some other consideration?

Another court was subsequently asked to determine whether the word *aunt* belonged in the same category as *mother* and *daughter*. If the prior court based its reasoning on the number of syllables in a word, then the word *aunt* would not belong in the category. Based on the reasoning of the prior court, the critical fact in this scenario is two-syllable words. Unlike the words *daughter* and *mother*, which consist of two syllables, *aunt* consists of only one and would not belong in the same category.

If the prior court, however, reasoned that only words that represent the same gender belong in the category, then the word *aunt* would belong. The word *aunt* would be consistent with the court's reasoning. Based on this reasoning, the critical fact in this scenario are words that represent the same gender. Like the words *daughter* and *mother*, which represent females, the word *aunt* also represents females and belongs in the category.

The above example illustrates the importance of identifying the court's reasoning in order to identify the critical facts. Although the words *mother, daughter,* and *aunt* could be categorized in at least two ways, by the number of syllables or by gender, you cannot identify the critical facts without first understanding the reasoning of the court. The court's reasoning determines which facts in a case are critical.

Students sometimes attempt to make analogies to any similar fact shared by both the precedent and the case-at-bar. This strategy is problematic. *Stare decisis* will only apply when a prior case is legally analogous to the case-at-bar. A case is legally analogous when the critical facts or some characteristic of the critical facts are similar. Basing a fact comparison on a non-critical fact, by merely pointing to a random fact similarity, is not a legally persuasive analogy. Consider the following arguments derived from the *Cane* case:

> **Argument 1**: Like the defendant in *Cane*, who carried liability insurance, the defendant in the present case also carried liability insurance.

> **Argument 2**: Like the defendant in *Cane* who was liable when she touched the plaintiff with her cane, our defendant touched the plaintiff with his umbrella.

The first argument is unpersuasive, because it compares a non-critical fact. Whether the defendant in *Cane* carried liability insurance had no bearing on the ultimate disposition of the case. The second argument is persuasive, because it does compare the critical facts.

Some students may also be tempted to compare the holding or conclusion of a case instead of comparing the critical facts. This analysis is illogical. Analogical analysis compares the facts of a decided case to the facts of your case. An argument should not compare a conclusion, instead it should compare facts that compel a conclusion. Comparing conclusions does not show the court why it must rule in a particular way. It only shows that you are seeking a particular result. Consider the following arguments derived from the *Cane* case:

> **Argument 1**: The Court should find the defendant liable, because like the defendant in *Cane*, who was liable when she touched the plaintiff with her cane, our defendant touched the plaintiff with his umbrella.

> **Argument 2**: The Court should find in favor of the plaintiff, because like the defendant in *Cane* who was

liable to the plaintiff, our defendant is also liable to the plaintiff.

The second argument is unpersuasive. Instead of comparing critical facts, it merely requests a particular result. The lawyer is merely asking the court to find in favor of the plaintiff because some other case also found in favor of a plaintiff. The lawyer is not demonstrating any reason why the court is required, under *stare decisis,* to follow the precedent.

The first argument is more persuasive. Here, the lawyer identified the critical fact and compared it to the facts of her case. The lawyer is arguing that the *Cane* holding must apply because the key facts, a cane and an umbrella, are similar. Therefore, under *stare decisis*, the court should also find that the defendant is liable to the plaintiff.

Unlike the *Cane* example, cases rarely turn on one critical fact derived from one case. Comprehensive analysis requires an examination of all the critical facts in a precedent. Courts usually weigh a variety of sometimes disparate facts when reaching a decision. Some controlling authority may include both favorable facts and damaging facts. In these situations, the court may conclude that one fact or a group of facts outweighs others. Careful and repeated readings of the cases help lawyers differentiate highly material facts from less material facts of a particular legal issue.

Moreover, the *Cane* example analyzed only one case. Sophisticated legal analysis, however, rarely relies on one precedent. Often lawyers analyze a number of cases, analogizing to some while distinguishing others. One technique that allows lawyers to analyze several cases at once is called *case synthesis*. Case synthesis permits lawyers to incorporate an entire body of law in a concise and comprehensive analysis.

2. Case Synthesis

Case synthesis is related to rule synthesis previously discussed in Chapter 2. Both skills require an examination of the body of case law that addresses a particular issue. Rule synthesis blends several cases to form one holistic rule. Case synthesis blends several cases to identify a common denominator among the precedents that can serve as the basis of an analogy.

In some instances, courts state a holding without expressly articulating the reasoning that justified the holding. In other instances, courts state the reasoning, but not clearly. Moreover, for many issues, lawyers find numerous opinions that are on-point. While the number of cases may seem overwhelming, case synthesis provides an effective tool for lawyers to integrate a large body of case law into one holistic analysis. It helps lawyers identify the common denominator among the precedents and streamlines the body of law into a workable cornerstone of analysis.

To synthesize several cases, lawyers carefully read the applicable opinions that are relevant to an issue, and identify the critical facts, holdings, reasoning, and any rules articulated. They also search for a common denominator, or thread among the critical facts of the different opinions, that incorporates the holdings and reasoning of the various precedents. Finally, lawyers blend the relevant opinions in order to incorporate all the holdings of the applicable authority. Case synthesis allows attorneys to organize the analysis around the common denominator derived from the precedents, instead of organizing the analysis around individual cases.

Case synthesis requires extrapolating the common significance among the critical facts of several cases. Identify the common thread among the cases by extrapolating the critical facts from the numerous precedents until some commonality is identified. This commonality should be a characteristic that is shared by the critical facts in all of the precedents. The commonality found, however, must be germane to the reasoning and holdings of the precedents.

To uncover the commonality, brainstorm to find the first level of similarity between the critical facts in the precedents and the case-at-bar. List the characteristics of the critical facts, abstracting from the specific to the general. Each abstraction should eliminate a specific trait. The common characteristic found between the facts in the precedents and the facts in the case-at-bar could provide the basis of an analogy.

Sample Case Synthesis

You are an Assistant District Attorney. The Defendant is charged with receiving stolen property. She is challenging the police's search and seizure of a handwritten note she posted on a bulletin board in a public library. The note advertised the sale of a car and listed the Defendant's name and phone number. The Defendant knew the car was stolen. The police seized the note in order to prove that the Defendant possessed the stolen car, an element of the offense. The Defendant claims that the police violated her Fourth Amendment right against unreasonable searches and seizures.

Your research revealed the following opinions:

> **Case A:** The defendant cannot challenge the government's seizure of garbage that he discarded for collection. Under the Fourth Amendment, the defendant had no reasonable expectation of privacy with respect to the garbage. To challenge a search and seizure under the Fourth Amendment, a defendant must have a reasonable expectation of privacy concerning the place searched or the object seized.

> **Case B:** Police dogs smelled the defendant's luggage in an airport and found drugs. The smell of the defendant's luggage in the public airport, however, did not violate his Fourth Amendment right. The defendant did not have a reasonable expectation of privacy concerning the smell of his luggage, because anyone in the airport could have smelled it.

To synthesize these cases, identify the common denominator among the precedents and the case-at-bar. The common denominator must relate to the holdings and reasoning, if articulated, in the authority. In the above example, review the critical facts to identify the common denominator.

Critical Facts	
Case A:	Discarded Garbage
Case B:	Smell of Luggage in Airport
Case-at-Bar:	Note Posted in Public Library

Identify the common thread among these dissimilar critical facts that relate to the holdings of the opinions. Extrapolate the critical facts in Cases A and B. At each level eliminate a specific characteristic until you reach a general characteristic that is shared by the critical fact found in the other case.

Consider the following:

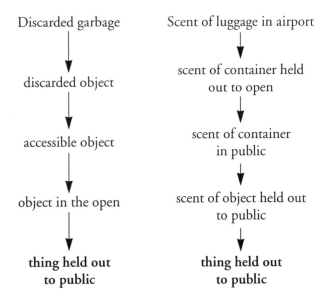

In the example above, some measure of intellectual flexibility is required in order to discover the commonality between the objects. The commonality between Cases A and B could be that persons have no reasonable expectation of privacy in *things held out to the public*. This commonality, then, can become the basis of an analogy.

Employing case synthesis, the Defendant in the case-at-bar does not have a reasonable expectation of privacy in a note she posted in a public library, a thing held out to the public. Like the discarded garbage in Case A and the smell from luggage in Case B, the Defendant in the present case does not have a reasonable expectation of privacy in the note, because it is also a thing held out to the public.

B. Analogical Strategies

Lawyers utilize critical facts and case synthesis when employing analogical strategies. This section focuses on two analogical strategies: the narrow analogy and the broad analogy. The narrow analogy focuses on direct fact comparisons between the precedent and the case-at-bar, while broad analogies focus on the significance of those facts.

Analogical Strategies

---

1. Narrow Analogy
2. Broad Analogy

---

1. Narrow Analogy

One analytical strategy, *narrow analogy*, largely depends on finding direct or substantial similarities and distinctions between facts of your case and the facts of the controlling authority. Utilizing a narrow analogy, lawyers seek to persuade a court that their client should prevail because the controlling case law has substantially similar facts to the facts of the case-at-bar. After the similarity is identified and the reasoning of the precedent is applied to the facts of your case, the argument concludes that the court should reach the same holding as the precedent or, by implication, risk violating *stare decisis*.

Alternatively, lawyers also use narrow analogies to distinguish the facts of the case-at-bar from the precedent. Here, lawyers argue that the key facts of the precedent are distinguishable from the case-at-bar. This argument implies that the court is not obliged to follow *stare decisis* because the facts are not analogous, thus the precedent should have no bearing on the outcome of the case. Whether drawing distinctions or similarities, narrow analogies examine the critical facts of the controlling case law and compare those facts with the facts of the case-at-bar.

When drafting an argument, the objective is to persuade a court that the controlling authority is either analogous to the case-at-bar and *stare decisis* should be followed, or that the controlling authority is factually dissimilar to the case-at-bar and *stare decisis* should not be followed. Once you determine that narrow analogy is appropriate, follow four steps to formulate your argument: (1) state the point of the analysis; (2) state the direct or narrow fact comparison, (3) apply the court's reasoning, and (4) conclude.

The Four-Step Argument: Narrow Analogy

Step One: State the Point of the Analysis.
Step Two: State the **Narrow** fact comparison.
Step Three: Apply the court's reasoning to your case.
Step Four: Conclude.

---

a. Step One — State the Point of the Analysis

The first step in formulating an argument is to state the point of the analysis. The point sentence introduces the reader to the topic of the analysis. If the analysis compares the critical facts in only one case, the point sentence should introduce that case and the point of law analyzed. The point sentence can also identify whether the case analyzed is analogous or distinguishable to the case-at-bar. Legal analysis, however, rarely turns on one case. If the analysis compares the facts of several cases, then the point sentence should state the synthesized commonality derived from the authority. Stating the point sentence of the analysis is similar to stating the topic sentence of a paragraph.

Consider the following examples of point sentences derived from the *Cane* example:

Argument 1: The instrumentality used to inflict harm in *Cane* is analogous to the instrumentality used to inflict harm in the case-at-bar.

Argument 2: The plaintiff will prevail.

The second argument is not a point sentence, it is merely a conclusion. That sentence did not introduce the topic of the analysis or identify if the law applies to the case-at-bar. The first argument, however, is a point sentence. It identified the case law and the general premise of the analysis. The point sentence stated that the cited authority is factually analogous to the case-at-bar. The argument, however, relied on only one case. If several cases are relevant, then the point sentence should clearly identify whether the body of law is analogous or distinguishable from the case-at-bar.

Suppose the *Cane* analysis relied on several cases. While the facts and holdings of the cases differed, the court consistently reasoned that instrumentalities used to inflict harm can support an action in tort. Under this scenario, the point sentence may read:

The instrumentalities of harm in *Cane*, *Smith*, and *Howard* are analogous to the instrumentality of harm in the case-at-bar.

b. Step Two — State the Narrow Fact Comparison

The second step in formulating an argument is to state the fact comparison. Here, lawyers assert how the critical facts in the case-at-bar compare to the critical facts already identified in the controlling precedent. The fact comparison should be clear, precise, and significant. The goal is to select a fact that bears on the ultimate disposition of the precedent. That fact should directly relate to the reasoning of the court. When stating the narrow fact comparison, point to specific facts rather than loose generalizations or tenuous characterizations.

Consider the following narrow fact comparisons derived from the *Cane* example:

Argument 1: The instrumentality used to inflict harm in *Cane* is analogous to the instrumentality used to inflict harm in the case-at-bar. **Like the defendant in Cane, who was liable when he harmed the plaintiff, the defendant in the present case also harmed the plaintiff.**

Argument 2: The instrumentality used to inflict harm in *Cane* is analogous to the instrumentality used to inflict harm in the case-at-bar. **Like the defendant in Cane, who was liable when he hit the plaintiff with a cane, the defendant in the present case also hit the plaintiff, but with an umbrella.**

The first argument is unpersuasive because the fact comparison is unclear, imprecise, and not related to the reasoning of the precedent. The *Cane* case considered whether the defendant harmed another with an instrumentality within his control. Merely arguing that both defendants harmed the respective plaintiffs, without specifying how, will not convince the court to follow the prior decision. The analogy should instead focus on the instrumentality of harm, rather than the harm itself.

The second argument is more persuasive. It compares instrumentalities within the control of the respective defendants. It likens a *cane* to an *umbrella*. The persuasiveness of a analysis, however, will turn on the applicability of the comparison to the reasoning of the precedent.

c.　Step Three—Apply the Court's Reasoning

The third step of narrow analogy explains the reasoning of the precedent and its applicability to the fact comparison. Merely pointing to a fact similarity, or distinction, by itself, is inadequate. To sufficiently argue a point of law, lawyers must not only persuade the court that the precedent's reasoning applies to the case-at-bar, but also how it applies.

To demonstrate that a fact was dispositive in a case, lawyers must prove that the fact comparison relates to the court's reasoning. In step two, the fact comparison merely laid out the similarities or differences between the precedent and the case-at-bar. Without explaining why that comparison is legally significant, lawyers are not showing how the critical facts relate to the law.

Remember that a fact comparison is a double-edged sword. It can be used either to draw analogies or distinctions depending on the lawyer's legal position. The distinction or analogy unfolds when lawyers demonstrate how the fact comparison relates to the reasoning of the precedent.

Consider the following arguments derived from the *Cane* example:

Argument 1: The instrumentality used to inflict harm in *Cane* is analogous to the instrumentality used to inflict harm in the case-at-bar. Like the defendant in the *Cane* case, who was liable when he hit the plaintiff with a cane, the defendant in the present case also hit the plaintiff, but with an umbrella. **The *Cane* court reasoned that an instrumentality within the direct control of a defendant can form the basis of common-law battery when that instrumentality is an extension of the bearer's arm.** An umbrella, like a cane, is also an extension of the bearer's arm and within his direct control.

Argument 2: The instrumentality used to inflict harm in *Cane* is analogous to the instrumentality used to inflict harm in the case-at-bar. Unlike the defendant in the *Cane* case who was liable when he hit the plaintiff with a cane, the defendant in the present case hit the plaintiff, but with an umbrella. **The *Cane* court reasoned that an instrumentality within the direct control of a defendant can form the basis of common-law battery when that instrumentality is an extension of the bearer's arm. While a cane is within the direct control of the bearer, an umbrella is not. An umbrella is susceptible to the forces of rain and wind.**

This example illustrates how to use the court's reasoning to support your argument. It also demonstrates how the same case can be used to support either party's position. A *cane* and an *umbrella* have both similar and different characteristics. The similarities and differences, however, must relate to the reasoning of the precedent.

d.   Step Four—Conclude

The fourth and final step of a narrow analogy completes the argument. The conclusion typically reminds the court of the general demand for relief. The logical progression of the argument culminates with a conclusion.

Review both the plaintiff's and the defendant's argument in their entirety:

> **Argument 1:** The instrumentality of harm in *Cane* is analogous to the instrumentality of harm in the case-at-bar. Like the defendant in the *Cane* case, who was liable when he hit the plaintiff with a cane, the defendant in the present case also hit the plaintiff, but with an umbrella. The *Cane* court reasoned that an instrumentality within the direct control of a defendant can form the basis of common-law battery when that instrumentality is an extension of the bearer's arm. An umbrella, like a cane, is also an extension of the bearer's arm and within his direct control. **The Court should hold that the defendant is liable for common-law battery.**

> **Argument 2:** The instrumentality of harm in *Cane* is not analogous to the instrumentality of harm in the case-at-bar. Unlike the defendant in the *Cane* case, who was liable when he hit the plaintiff with a cane, the defendant in the present case hit the plaintiff with an umbrella. The *Cane* court reasoned that an instrumentality within the direct control of a defendant can form the basis of common-law battery when that instrumentality is an extension of the bearer's arm. While a cane is within the direct control of the bearer, an umbrella is not. An umbrella is susceptible to the

forces of rain and wind. **The Court should hold that the defendant is not liable for common-law battery.**

Keep in mind the *Cane* example involved only one issue, one case, and the application of only one critical fact. Legal analysis, however, rarely relies on one argument derived from one precedent. Typically, lawyers make arguments from a number of cases, analogizing to some while distinguishing others.

A narrow analogy is only one method of analyzing the law and devising an effective legal argument. Narrow analogies focus on direct fact comparisons between a precedent and the case-at-bar. The analogy is supported by the proposition that courts are bound to follow decisions that have already decided the same legal issue under the same or similar facts. Some cases, however, are not amenable to a narrow analogy. These cases might require a broader analytical strategy. By understanding that legal analysis is not limited to one approach, you will not limit the strength or sophistication of your analysis.

2.   Broad Analogy

Although narrow analogies are effective in many cases, a broader analogical strategy may be more appropriate when the relationship between the critical facts in the precedent and the case-at-bar are tenuous. Narrow analogies compare specific critical facts in the controlling authority that are closely parallel to facts in the case-at-bar. This analytical approach requires attorneys to draw narrow comparisons focused on material facts. In contrast, the broad analogy draws general comparisons that relate to, but are not necessarily parallel to, the critical facts. The basis of the broad analogy is not the critical fact itself, but rather the common denominator derived from the critical facts in the precedents. As previously discussed, case synthesis is the process that identifies the common denominator among various precedents. Broad analogies require some measure of intellectual flexibility in order to devise persuasive arguments that incorporate less obvious comparisons.

There are two situations when broad analogies are appropriate. First, broad analogies are appropriate when the case-at-bar arises under unique or unusual facts. These cases may not have the factual characteristics necessary for a narrow analogy, because facts of the cases may not be amenable to a direct fact comparison. Second, broad analogies are appropriate when the analysis requires the integration of a large body of law. Often, lawyers must synthesize several cases in order to identify a basis of an analogy.

Like narrow analogies, broad analogies also require a close examination of the court's reasoning. Merely identifying some characteristic common to both a critical fact in the precedents and the case-at-bar is not persuasive. The comparison must be relevant to the underlying reasoning of the court.

The broad analogy compares the common characteristic of the facts in the precedents to the case-at-bar the same way the narrow analogy compares the specific critical facts in the precedents to the case-at-bar. Once you determine that broad analogy is appropriate, follow the following four steps to formulate your argument: (1) state the point of the analysis; (2) state the broad comparison, (3) apply the court's reasoning, and (4) conclude. These steps are identical to the four step argument used for the narrow analogy, except Step Two focuses on a broad, as opposed to a narrow, comparison.

The Four-Step Argument: Broad Analogy

Step One: State the Point of the Analysis.
Step Two: State the **Broad** comparison.
Step Three: Apply the court's reasoning to your case.
Step Four: Conclude.

Consider the following example:

Your client, the plaintiff, dug a well on the defendant's property. The plaintiff claims she owns the land through adverse possession. Adverse possession is a legal doctrine that awards ownership of property to a possessor who openly, actually, exclusively, adversely, notoriously, and continuously possesses the land of another for twenty years. The only issue is whether your client can establish actual use, one element of adverse possession. You find the following opinions:

Case A — The plaintiff has not shown adverse possession of the defendant's property because she failed to satisfy the actual use test. Adverse possessors must demonstrate actual use of the property in order to establish ownership through adverse possession. Actual use is demonstrated by acts of dominion and control by the adverse possessor. The plaintiff placed a picnic table and shade umbrella on the defendant's property. This use did not establish dominion and control.

Case B — The plaintiff has demonstrated ownership of the property through adverse possession. Adverse possession is established when an adverse possessor demonstrates dominion and control over the contested property. The plaintiff built a three-story brick house on the locus. This structure did show dominion and control.

Case C — The plaintiff has established adverse possession. The adverse possessor must show actual use of the adversely possessed property. Actual use is best shown by evidence of dominion and control over the property. The plaintiff built an in-ground swimming pool on the locus and placed numerous beach chairs around the perimeter of the pool. While the beach chairs are not evidence of dominion and control because they are easily removable from the locus, the in-ground pool is evidence of dominion and control because it is not easily removable from the locus.

To analyze whether the plaintiff satisfies the actual use element of adverse possession, first, identify the critical facts; those facts that were dispositive to the courts' holdings. In Case A, the critical facts include a picnic table and shade umbrella. In Case B, the critical fact is a three-story brick house. In Case C, the critical facts are an in-ground swimming pool and lounge chairs.

Second, identify the holdings and reasoning of the authority. The court held that the plaintiffs in Cases B and C satisfied the actual use test of adverse possession because a house and an in-ground swimming pool demonstrated the dominion and control of property. Moreover, Case C suggested that improvements that are not easily removable from the property satisfy the actual use test for adverse possession. The plaintiff in case A failed to show adverse possession because a picnic table and shade umbrella did not establish dominion and control of the property.

Third, identify the commonality between all the critical facts of the controlling authority that demonstrate the significance of these facts as they relate to the holdings and reasoning of the authority. Lawyers can discern the commonality by extrapolating the common denominator among the critical facts, paying close attention to the significance the courts gave to the characteristics of the facts.

Under the cases described above, a brick house and an in-ground swimming pool demonstrated dominion and control of the property. On the other hand, a picnic table, a shade umbrella, and lounge chairs did not exhibit dominion and control of the property. What is the common characteristic that is present or absent from these facts?

In Case C, the court opined that lounge chairs are not evidence of actual use because they are easily removable from the property. Conversely, an in-ground swimming pool is evidence of actual use because it is not easily removable from the property. By extrapolating these facts together with the facts of the other cases, a common denominator that furthers the reasoning of the authority can be identified that ties the cases together.

Using the court's reasoning, identify the thread that ties all the cases together. An in-ground swimming pool, and, by analogy, a brick house, demonstrated dominion and control because they were not easily removable from the locus. They are not easily removable because they are *permanent improvements* or changes to property. A shade umbrella, lounge chairs, and a picnic table did not demonstrate dominion and control because they were easily removable from the locus. They were easily removable from the locus because they were not *permanent improvements* to property. The significance of the critical facts, namely their permanent or temporary character, is the common denominator that can form the basis of a broad analogy.

Employing a broad analytical strategy, a lawyer may draft an argument in the following manner:

> The improvements made in Case B and Case C are analogous to the improvements made in the present case. Like the adverse possessors in Cases B and C, who made permanent improvements to the locus, the plaintiff also made permanent improvements to the locus. The courts have reasoned that actual use is demonstrated by dominion and control. Dominion and control is shown by evidence of permanent improvements that are not easily removable from the locus. The plaintiff dug a well on the property. Like the brick house in Case B and the in-ground swimming pool in Case C, the well is also evidence of dominion and control because it is not easily removable from the property. Moreover, unlike the picnic table and shade umbrella in Case A which were easily removable from the property, a well is not. The Court should rule that the plaintiff has satisfied actual use, an element of adverse possession.

Even though a well, a swimming pool, and a shade umbrella are not readily comparable, finding a common characteristic that is consistent with the court's reasoning can be used to devise effective legal arguments. In this example, a permanent improvement to property was the common characteristic shared by all the critical facts. A well, swimming pool, and a brick house are all permanent improvements to property. This characteristic also comports with the reasoning articulated by the court. The court ruled that dominion and control demonstrates actual use, one element of adverse possession. The court reasoned that improvements that are easily removable from the property do not satisfy actual use. Permanent improvements are, by definition, not easily removable and, thus, could satisfy the actual use requirement.

The different methods or strategies discussed in this book are not an exhaustive discussion of every possible approach to legal analysis. Narrow analogies and broad analogies are similar analytical strategies. Both use the court's reasoning and compare facts. The difference is the specificity of the facts compared. Narrow analogy compares closely parallel facts, while a broad analogy compares more general commonalities. Deciding which strategy to use depends on the precedent, the specific issues raised, and the facts in your case.

Understanding narrow and broad analogies is an important step in developing the skills necessary to become an effective advocate. Bear in mind that these strategies are not mutually exclusive. In fact, attorneys often incorporate variations of both analogies in a single argument. Also note that a wide variety of analytical strategies exist. Most of these techniques, however, are usually variations of the concepts discussed in this book. With practice, students can use these strategies and develop the expertise necessary to devise sophisticated analysis on any legal issue.

Practice Exercises

Complete the following exercises to reinforce your understanding of this chapter:

1. Define critical facts.

2. How do lawyers identify critical facts in a case?

3. How can both the plaintiff and the defendant use the same precedent to support their arguments?

4. When is it appropriate to use narrow analogies?

5. When is it appropriate to use broad analogies?

6. Why is it important to compare precedent to your client's case?

7. Consider the following opinion:

   The Defendant and his roommate got into an argument. The Defendant then lit a cigarette and used it to burn his roommate's arm by holding him down and thrusting the cigarette into his arm eight times. Held: the Defendant is guilty of assault and battery with a dangerous weapon.

   An assault and battery with a dangerous weapon is a criminal battery inflicted with an inherently dangerous weapon, or an object used as a weapon in a dangerous or potentially dangerous way. Some inherently dangerous objects, such as a gun or knife, designed to inflict serious bodily harm or death, are presumptively dangerous weapons. Other objects may still be considered dangerous if they are used in a dangerous or potentially dangerous manner. Considering the manner that the lighted cigarette was handled and controlled by the defendant, and the violent circumstances of the assault, we hold that the lighted cigarette was used as a dangerous weapon. Therefore, the Defendant is liable for assault and battery with a dangerous weapon.

   a. What are the critical facts of the opinion?
   b. What is the reasoning of the court?
   c. What is the holding of the court?

Your client is charged with assault and battery with a dangerous weapon. Your client was looking for a parking space in front of a store. She saw an empty parking space, and signaled with her directional to indicate that she was intending to pull into the space. Just before your client pulled into the space, another driver cut in front of your client with her car, and drove into the parking space. Your client then got out of her car and began to argue with the other driver. A scuffle ensued. Your client poked the other driver's eyes with her car keys.

   d. Draft the defendant's argument analyzing whether the court should hold that car keys are a dangerous weapon.
   e. Draft the prosecutor's argument analyzing whether the court should hold that car keys are a dangerous weapon.

8. Your client was charged with arson. You find one precedent on-point. That court articulated a four-part test for arson. That test requires: 1) the intentional or reckless disregard of an apparent risk, 2) burning, 3) of a dwelling, 4) of another. The only element at issue was whether the element of burning was satisfied. The facts of that case revealed that a defendant started a fire that caused the charring of two walls in a building. The court held that charring was sufficient to satisfy the burning element. The court reasoned that some damage to the structure caused by fire is required. The court noted that substantial damage or destruction of the structure is not required to commit arson.

In your client's case, the only issue is whether the burning element is satisfied. Your client threw a match into a waste-paper basket. The basket smouldered and while smoke blackened the walls in the building, the walls were not charred. The heat from the fire activated the fire sprinklers which doused the fire.

    a. Draft an argument analyzing why the burning element of arson is not satisfied.

    b. Draft an argument analyzing why the burning element of arson is satisfied.

9. You are prosecuting a defendant for receiving stolen property. Your research reveals that the elements of receiving stolen property are: 1) possession and control, 2) of stolen property, 3) known to be stolen, 4) by another, 5) with intent to permanently deprive the owner of the property. Your research uncovers a precedent concluding that even though that defendant did not manually possess the stolen property, the defendant still possessed stolen property when he instructed another to place it in a location that the defendant selected.

In your case, you are prosecuting the defendant for receiving stolen property. The defendant used a telephone to fence stolen property. Fencing is when one arranges, for the thief, the sale of stolen property to another. The defendant never physically possessed the property. The only issue in your case is whether the defendant possessed the property.

    a. Draft the prosecutor's argument analyzing why the possession element is satisfied.

    b. Draft the defendant's argument analyzing why the possession element is not satisfied.

10. Consider the following opinion:

Presenting the defendant with a diamond ring, the plaintiff asked the defendant to marry him. She agreed. The defendant later broke the engagement. We hold that the plaintiff can reclaim the engagement ring. We reason that the plaintiff should recover because the defendant broke the engagement.

a. What are the critical facts of the opinion?

b. What is the reasoning of the court?

c. What is the holding of the court?

Your client, the plaintiff, was engaged to be married to the defendant. The defendant later broke the engagement with your client. The plaintiff wants to recover the diamond stud earrings that he bought the defendant a month before their intended wedding. He bought her the earrings to wear on her wedding day.

d. Draft the plaintiff's argument.

e. Can you predict how defense attorneys will distinguish the precedent? Draft the defense's argument.

11. Consider the following opinion:

The defendant was charged with involuntary manslaughter. The defendant found a revolver in an alley and brought it to work to show his friends. He did not check to see if the revolver was loaded. In jest, he pointed the revolver at a co-worker and pulled the trigger. The gun fired and killed his co-worker. We hold that the defendant is guilty of involuntary manslaughter. We reason that the defendant is guilty because a death resulted from the defendant's wanton and reckless conduct. A reasonable person standing in the shoes of the defendant would recognize the risk to human life.

a. What are the critical facts of the opinion?

b. What is the reasoning of the court?

c. What is the holding of the opinion?

Your client, a building manager, has been charged with involuntary manslaughter. A number of weeks ago, she locked the fire exit in the building she manages, hoping to prevent a rash of burglaries in the building. That night, a fire broke out in the building. Many residents were unable to escape because of the locked fire exit. One resident died of smoke inhalation.

    d. Which strategy, narrow or broad analogy, would be most effective here?

    e. Draft your client's legal argument.

Chapter 4

Statutory Analysis

OBJECTIVES

WHEN YOU FINISH READING THIS CHAPTER AND COMPLETE THE
EXERCISES YOU WILL BE ABLE TO:

- RECOGNIZE THE ROLE OF STATUTES;
- INTERPRET STATUTES;
- APPLY STATUTES TO LEGAL PROBLEMS.

Chapter 1 introduced two sources of law: statutes and case
law. Chapter 3 explained how to analyze case law. This chapter
explains how to analyze statutes.

Case-law analysis often requires lawyers to identify a rule by
synthesizing many cases. In contrast to case-law analysis, statutory analysis begins with the rule, the statute itself. The rule is the
focus of the analysis. Statutory analysis may also require the examination of other sources to interpret the meaning and application of that rule.

Statutory analysis uses analytical strategies similar to case-law
analysis, but examines statutes together with case law. Statutory
analysis involves two steps. First, lawyers construe the statute to
determine its meaning. Second, lawyers apply the statute to the
legal problem.

Statutory Analysis

Step One: Construe the Statute
Step Two: Apply the Statute to Your Case

A. Step One—Construing the Statute

Courts interpret statutes consistent with, and to effectuate, the legislature's intent. That intent, however, may be difficult to identify. Therefore, courts apply several rules of statutory construction in order to identify the legislature's intent. Consequently, to properly analyze a statute, lawyers must first understand how a court will construe it. This chapter examines three concepts of statutory construction: the plain meaning doctrine; mandatory vs. discretionary statutes; and ambiguous statutes.

Statutory Construction

---

1. Plain Meaning Doctrine
2. Mandatory vs. Discretionary Statutes
3. Ambiguous Statutes

---

1. The Plain Meaning Doctrine

Statutory construction begins by examining the text of a statute. When construing a statute, courts first look to the *plain meaning* of the statutory language. When a statute is unambiguous, courts must give the language its plain meaning. The plain meaning is the meaning of a word or phrase that is generally accepted by reasonable persons.

If a court were to strictly interpret a statute according to its plain meaning, but that interpretation would have an illogical result or frustrate the legislature's intent, then the court may disregard the statute's plain meaning. This exception to the plain meaning doctrine prevents a literal interpretation that ignores logic and fairness.

Suppose a statute stated that an alleged shoplifter may not prevail on a false imprisonment claim against a shopkeeper if (1) a reasonable man would believe that the shoplifter was committing the offense of shoplifting *or* (2) the manner of the detention or arrest by a shopkeeper and the length of time the shopper was detained was reasonable. The issue before the court was whether both elements (1) and (2) must be satisfied or whether either element, alone, is sufficient to establish false imprisonment.

Suppose the court, construing the statute, interpreted the word *"or"* as the conjunctive *"and,"* requiring that *both* statutory elements be satisfied, instead of *either* element. The court might disregard the plain meaning of the word "or," because it would lead to an illogical result. If a merchant had reasonable grounds to suspect a person of shoplifting, but then locked that person in a stockroom for twenty-two hours, the plaintiff should prevail on a claim of false imprisonment. Denying the plaintiff a cause of action merely because only one element was satisfied would be absurd and contrary to legislative intent. Thus, the court may disregard the plain meaning of statutory language to ensure a logical result.

2. Mandatory vs. Discretionary Statutes

When reading statutes, lawyers pay close attention to each word. They pay particular attention to words such as *"shall"* and *"may."* The word *shall* determines whether the statute or part of the statute requires mandatory compliance. The word *may* determines whether compliance is discretionary.

Suppose a statute states that the State *may* renew contracts for construction of the state's highways for two years. With the discretionary *may*, the state has the discretion to renew the contract. Now suppose the statute states that the State *shall* renew contracts for construction of the state's highways for two years. Using the mandatory *shall*, the state must renew the contract.

Other language that may indicate whether compliance with a statute or part of a statute is mandatory or discretionary is the use of the conjunctions *"and"* and *"or."* The conjunction *"and"* signifies that the parts of a statute are mandatory, or required. In contrast, the conjunction *"or"* signifies that parts of a statute are discretionary.

Mandatory Language   *Shall, Must, Required, And*
Discretionary Language *May, Either, Or*

3. Ambiguous Statutes

When creating a law, legislators make every effort to choose language that clearly conveys the statute's meaning and purpose. The statutory language, however, is often ambiguous or vague. A statute is ambiguous when the language is susceptible to more than one meaning. A statute is vague when language is stated in indefinite terms.

Consider the following statute: It is illegal to possess weapons in school. This statute is vague in several ways. The word *weapons* is an indefinite term. It is unclear whether the legislature intended to prohibit guns, knives, scissors, or some other instrument. The word *school* is also vague because it is unclear whether the legislature intended to prohibit weapons in public schools, private schools, or both. In order to answer these questions, lawyers must determine what the legislature intended when it enacted the statute.

When a statute is ambiguous, courts utilize various sources of legislative intent to determine the meaning of the statute. Sources of legislative intent include (a) maxims of statutory construction, (b) legislative history, and (c) cases. Without clearly understanding the meaning of a statute, you cannot determine if its provisions apply to your case.

Sources of Legislative Intent
a. Maxims
b. Legislative History
c. Cases Construing Statutes

a. Maxims

There are several maxims that aid a court in determining the legislative intent of statutes. Among these are *in pari materia* and *ejusdem generis*. Understanding these maxims and the role they play in statutory construction help lawyers predict how courts will interpret statutes.

In pari materia is a Latin phrase meaning "on like subject matter." Statutes that are *in pari materia* should be read consistently with each other. This maxim requires courts to construe sections or parts of statutes harmoniously with each other, as well as sections or parts in other statutes on the same subject or with the same purpose. This maxim ensures harmony within the body of legislative law by requiring coherence among similar provisions. The court examines the whole statutory scheme even when considering only one section. Courts will even consider other legislative schemes in order to maintain consistency among the entire corpus of statutes.

Suppose one section of the Insurance Code states that an insurer will only reimburse the insured for required medical treatment. Another section of the Insurance Code states that a face lift is elective surgery. A court construing both statutes *in pari materia* would prohibit the insured from getting reimbursed for a face lift. A facelift, an elective procedure, would not be reimbursed, because it is not a required medical treatment. That court would construe the two sections of the Insurance Code consistently with each other.

Another maxim, *ejusdem generis,* is a Latin phrase meaning "of the same kind." When a general word follows a list of specific examples, the general term should be construed to include only things of the same type as those specified in the list. This maxim limits the court's interpretative freedom by restricting the scope of statutory language.

Suppose a statute states that restaurants are not liable for lost coats, hats, umbrellas, or other personal items. Your client checked her briefcase with the coat check at a restaurant. When she went to retrieve her briefcase it was gone. She sued the restaurant for damages. A court utilizing *ejusdem generis* to construe the statute would determine whether a briefcase is considered the same type of personal items as those specifically listed in the statute.

b. Legislative History

Legislative history is useful in determining what the legislature intended when it enacted a statute. Legislative history is the paper trail of a bill as it works its way through the different stages in the legislative process. It is persuasive authority that attorneys and courts use to interpret the language of a statute.

By reviewing language in an original bill, one source of legislature history, and comparing it to the final statute, lawyers can determine the reason why the legislature enacted the law and why it used the particular language in the statute. Other sources of legislative history, such as transcripts of hearings, committee reports, proposed amendments, and debates, are also helpful in determining legislative intent.

c.   Cases Construing Statutes

Another way to determine legislative intent is to research and read cases that interpret statutes. *Stare decisis* and precedent, principles discussed in Chapter 1, are also applicable to statutory construction. Once a court determines the meaning of a statute, subsequent courts must follow that interpretation. Pursuant to *stare decisis*, a court's interpretation becomes precedent that other courts within its jurisdiction must follow. Although the legislature makes law by enacting statutes, courts also make law by interpreting a statute's meaning.

When construing a statute, courts can interpret statutory language broadly or narrowly. A broad interpretation gives expansive meaning to particular words or phrases in a statute. In contrast, a narrow interpretation strictly construes words or phrases. Courts may rely on legislative intent and policy considerations when determining whether the meaning of statutory language should be broadly or narrowly construed.

Consider the language of the following statute: Children are entitled to a share of their parent's estate unless they are expressly excluded from a will, and over eighteen years of age. In order to determine what the legislature intended by the word *children*, a review of applicable case law may be helpful. Previously, a court, attempting to effectuate the legislature's intent, broadly interpreted the word children to include both biological and adopted children. Pursuant to *stare decisis*, other courts in that jurisdiction must thereafter follow that case, including that court's interpretation of the statute.

B. Step Two—Application

Statutory analysis does not end after construing a statute's meaning. The next step is to apply the statute to your client's case. This step requires an application of each part, element, or definition in a statute to the facts of your case. Furthermore, if a court has interpreted the language or application of a statute, apply that interpretation to the facts in your client's case. To compare and contrast the cases to your client's case, utilize the methods of analysis discussed in Chapter 3, narrow analogies and broad analogies.

Review the following statute described above: Children are entitled to a share of their parent's estate unless they are expressly excluded from a will, and over eighteen years of age. Your client, a fourteen year-old boy, is the step-son of the deceased. He was expressly excluded from his step-father's will. He seeks your advice regarding the statute's applicability to his case.

Apply the statute to your client's case. Analyze each part of the statute in relation to the facts of his case. The statute appears to have three elements: (1) children, who are (2) expressly excluded from their parent's will, (3) and are over eighteen years of age. Our facts reveal that element two is met. The client's step-father did, in fact, expressly exclude him from his will. Our facts also reveal that element three is not met. The client is fourteen, well under the statute's prescribed age. One issue remains: whether element one is met. Specifically, the issue is whether a step-son falls within the class of *children*.

To resolve this final issue, review sources that interpret what the legislature intended by the word *children*. As you recall from above, a case already determined that adopted children are included within this class. To argue on behalf of your client, employ the analogical reasoning techniques discussed in Chapter 3.

This analysis would likely compare a step-child to an adopted child.

Statutory analysis involves many skills. Students must understand statutory construction and the application of a statute to a legal problem. Statutory analysis involves analyzing both statutes and cases. With the growing number of statutes in today's society, statutory analysis is increasingly important.

Practice Exercises

Complete the following exercises to reinforce your understanding of this chapter:

1. How is statutory analysis different than case-law analysis?

2. What are the two steps involved in statutory analysis?

3. Define the plain meaning doctrine.

4. What are three sources of legislative intent?

5. Define the maxim *in pari materia*.

6. Define the maxim *ejusdem generis*.

7. Complete the following questions regarding legislative history:

   a. Define legislative history.
   b. Name one source of legislative history that is helpful in determining legislative intent.

8. Consider the following statute: Defacing a library book is punishable by a $500 fine. Your client was caught underlining, in pencil, a word in a book she borrowed from her private school's library.

   a. Identify the issue.
   b. Can your client be fined under the statute?

9. A statute states: A burglary is a breaking and entering of a dwelling, at nighttime, with the intent to commit a felony therein. Your client broke a window and entered a houseboat at dusk with the intent to commit a felony. He has been charged with burglary.

   Will he be found guilty under the statute?

10. An anxious man just entered your office. He is concerned about a new law regarding child passenger restraints in vehicles. He owns a 1964 Corvette Stingray that does not have seat belts. He often takes his daughter for rides in the

Stingray. His daughter is five years-old and weighs thirty-five pounds.

The statute states: No child under the age of five and no child weighing forty pounds or less shall ride in a motor vehicle unless such child is correctly secured and fastened by a child passenger restraint. If said child is riding as a passenger in a motor vehicle made before 1962 that is not equipped with seat belts, the provisions of this statute do not apply.

He seeks your advice regarding the application of the law to his situation.

11. A statute prohibits the use of cigarettes, cigars, and other tobacco products, in state buildings. Would a court, employing *ejusdem generis,* determine that chewing tobacco is prohibited? Why?

Chapter 5

Policy

OBJECTIVES

WHEN YOU FINISH READING THIS CHAPTER AND COMPLETE THE
EXERCISES YOU WILL BE ABLE TO:

- DEFINE POLICY;
- EXPLAIN THE ROLE OF POLICY;
- DEVELOP POLICY ARGUMENTS.

This chapter explores policy and examines policy-based analysis. Policy is the purpose behind a law; it is the reason why courts or legislators make laws. Policy considers how the law impacts society. It considers the beneficial or injurious effects laws have on the well-being and prosperity of the community. Policies mirror the values of society. They protect and define the community's core principles.

Consider the policy underlying the crime of solicitation. Criminal solicitation occurs when someone requests, encourages, commands, or hires someone to commit a crime. The policy behind the crime of solicitation is two-fold. First, it protects members of society by preventing them from getting hurt by someone solicited to commit a crime. Second, it protects against members of society from being approached or induced by the solicitor to commit a crime. While the crime of solicitation prohibits specific acts by individuals, the policy behind the crime seeks to protect society as a whole.

Policy exists in both case law and statutes. In case law, courts often weigh policy considerations when deciding cases. Each judicial decision not only affects each party in a lawsuit, it also impacts the welfare of society as a whole. The policy that justifies the outcome of a particular case impacts everyone in that jurisdiction. Legislatures also carefully weigh policy considerations when enacting statutes. They enact laws to further the values and principles of their constituents.

A. Case Law

Policy in case law is generally identified by looking at the reasons why the court reached its holding. The reasoning of an opinion explains how a court reached its decision. If an opinion expressly articulates policy, you will generally find it in that part of the decision where the court justifies the outcome of the case. Here, the court may explain how the decision serves society's interest. If, however, a court's opinion does not expressly state policy, a review of prior cases may reveal policy concerns for that particular legal issue.

The following example illustrates how to identify policy in an opinion:

> *Commonwealth v. Defendant*—The defendant was charged with possession of illegal narcotics. He raised police entrapment as a defense. The facts reveal that an undercover police officer approached the defendant, gave him a sum of money, and asked him to purchase drugs on his behalf. The defendant declined. After persistent requests by the undercover officer, he finally agreed. When the defendant returned with the drugs, he was immediately arrested by the officer.
>
> Entrapment occurs when a government agent encourages a defendant to commit a crime and coerces that defendant to commit a crime he otherwise would

not have committed. This defendant is not guilty, because, but for the police action, the defendant would never have committed the crime. The entrapment defense exists to prevent police overreaching. Police officers should enforce the law, and not entice an otherwise law-abiding person into committing a crime. Police officers should never plant the seed of criminality in an innocent mind.

To identify policy in the above opinion, determine the court's reasoning in *Commonwealth v. Defendant.* The court reasoned that the defendant was not predisposed to commit the crime. Rather, he was coerced by the police. Where the court discusses its justification for its holding, it explains the policy underlying entrapment. The entrapment defense protects society by deterring police from abusing their power when they instigate members of society to commit crimes.

B. Statutes

Several sources identify policy in statutes. Sometimes the statute itself may expressly state the policy underlying a law. Other times, look at extrinsic sources of legislative intent. One source of legislative intent, the legislative history of a statute, can assist in determining the policy behind a statute. As discussed in Chapter 4, legislative history of a statute consists of the documents created as a bill advances through the different stages of the legislative process. A transcript of legislative hearings regarding a bill often reveals policy issues relevant to that bill.

Another source of legislative intent is cases that interpret a statute. When courts interpret statutes, they attempt to carry out the legislature's intent. To identify policy in statutes, identify the court's reasoning, looking for reasons why the court reached a particular decision. The court may discuss the statute's policy within the justification for its holding.

C. Policy Arguments

After identifying the policy, consider including policy arguments in the analysis of legal issues. Lawyers develop policy arguments to persuade the court to reach a desired outcome of the case. Policy arguments are typically used to bolster legal arguments. They are especially important when the facts or rules do not provide strong support for your position, or when the law is ambiguous or unsettled. Policy should be researched and analyzed in all legal problems, but especially in weaker cases. In some cases, policy may be your strongest argument.

Generally, lawyers use policy in six ways:

Six Uses of Policy
1. further existing policies,
2. analyze cases of first impression,
3. limit the scope of the law,
4. slightly expand the law,
5. analyze complex cases, and
6. evaluate competing policies.

1. Further Existing Policies

When possible, lawyers argue that the desired outcome furthers existing policies. Courts are conservative. They hesitate to make new law. An argument should demonstrate that your position promotes the existing policy. Policy defines the parameters of acceptable conduct. Therefore, policy arguments that fall outside those parameters will likely fail.

For example, the doctrine of adverse possession requires plaintiffs to possess another's property openly, exclusively, actually, adversely, notoriously, and continuously for twenty years. The policy behind this doctrine is to give property owners sufficient notice that another person is possessing the property owner's land.

Suppose Owner had five acres of wooded land behind his summer house. Possessor claims that he adversely possessed Owner's land for twenty years, off and on. Owner could make a persuasive legal argument that Possessor did not satisfy all of the elements of adverse possession. Possessor did not continuously possess the land for twenty years. Owner could bolster this argument by contending that his position fits squarely within the policy behind adverse possession. The policy is to provide sufficient notice to property owners. Owner did not have sufficient notice of his adverse possession, because Possessor did not continuously possess the property.

2. Analyze Cases of First Impression

While courts hesitate to make new law, cases of first impression may require the court to break new ground. Policy may play an important role when the court considers a case of first impression. A case of first impression is when courts have not yet resolved an issue, and thus, no precedent exists. In cases of first impression, policy may result in the recognition or adoption of legal doctrines.

When first considering a legal issue, courts will typically consider results that further the general purpose behind a law. They look to precedent for guidance. In cases of first impression, however, no binding law exists to guide the court. Lawyers use policy arguments to persuade courts to adopt new law, or take existing law in new directions.

Suppose in 1835, a court considered whether it should recognize common-law marriage as a valid form of marriage. The court looked at the policy implications of common-law marriage. It determined that the nature of the common-law marital relationship is necessary to protect individuals who could not otherwise comply with statutory marriage requirements. The court recognized that some pioneer communities did not have access to the means of statutory marriage. In order to protect couples who considered themselves married, but never complied with civil statutory marriage requirements, the court adopted common-law marriage. Policy considerations inspired the court's adoption of common-law marriage.

3. Limit the Scope of the Law

Policy can also be used to limit the law. Attorneys use policy to persuade courts to narrow the application of a law by arguing that the conditions that existed when the policy was first articulated no longer exist. Here, lawyers ask the court to construe the law narrowly, without abolishing it.

For example, in a case subsequent to the one discussed above, the court recognized that in contemporary society the pioneer conditions which stimulated the recognition of common-law marriages no longer exist. The court limited common-law marriage by only recognizing it when the parties at least attempt to satisfy statutory marriage requirements, but fail. Although the court limited the application of common-law marriage, it did not abolish it.

4. Slightly Expand the Law

While policy can be used to limit the law, attorneys also use policy to expand it. In some cases, an existing law fails to protect society, because it is too narrow. In these situations, attorneys use policy to persuade a court to expand the law to reflect current concerns of the public.

Consider a statute that first prohibited stalking. That statute stated that a person is guilty of stalking if a person intentionally and repeatedly follows or harasses another, and threatens that person with harm. Courts interpreting that statute have held defendants guilty of stalking when they followed victims on foot or with motor vehicles, or when they harassed the victim over the phone or through the mail. As computer technology has advanced, plaintiffs have commenced lawsuits that allege stalking over the Internet. Attorneys in these cases could make a policy argument to expand the court's interpretation of the stalking statute to include the Internet. This slight expansion should reflect current policy concerns that better address the public welfare.

5. Analyze Complex Cases

Attorneys also use policy arguments in complicated cases to provide courts with a simple resolution to complex legal issues. Sometimes, a case can be decided without resolving the intricacies of elaborate legal issues. Many federal constitutional issues, for example, are remarkably complicated. By keeping in mind the policy underlying the law, courts may use policy to steer through these complex constitutional issues. Although some cases involve many intricate issues and sub-issues that muddy the waters, policy may serve as a compass for courts when navigating difficult issues.

6. Evaluate Competing Policies

When analyzing legal issues, also consider and evaluate competing policy arguments. Some laws have policy interests that benefit each party's position. Courts weigh the interests of both parties, together with the public's interest, in order to resolve conflicting policy considerations. Therefore, it is important to anticipate your opponent's policy arguments.

For example, the highest court of appeals in a jurisdiction allowed bystanders to recover for negligent infliction of emotional distress. The distress must be caused by witnessing a defendant seriously injure a family member. The court reasoned that freedom from mental distress deserves legal protection. The court then weighed the competing policy considerations. The court considered the need to compensate plaintiffs whose emotional distress was caused by the defendant's negligence. This was weighed against the need to prevent unlimited liability of defendants, and the uncertainty in the law that would result if the court allowed recovery. The court also considered the general welfare of society. After weighing all the competing policy interests, the court concluded that it should not bar plaintiffs' causes of action.

Policy plays several different roles in legal analysis. It can be used to expand, limit, or create new law. Often overlooked, policy should be an important consideration in formulating legal arguments. While policy is not binding law, it may bolster an otherwise weak argument.

Practice Exercises

Complete the following exercises to reinforce your understanding of this chapter:

1. Define policy.

2. How do you identify policy in judicial opinions?

3. How do you identify policy in statutes?

4. List six uses of policy in persuasive arguments.

5. What is the policy behind the following requirements for a statutory marriage:
   a. Blood test for syphilis
   b. Obtaining a marriage license
   c. Waiting period between issuance of a license and the marriage ceremony
   d. Marriage ceremony attended by both the bride and groom and officiated by an authorized official

6. Identify the policy in the following precedent:

   The defendant decided to start a football pool in his office. He collected $20 from each of his ten co-workers who wanted to bet on a football game. He collected $200 in total. The plaintiff won the football bet, but the defendant refused to turn over the winnings. The plaintiff sued the defendant for breach of contract. The court held the plaintiff cannot recover, because gambling is illegal in the state.

7. What are the competing policy interests of a defendant's right to be protected from unreasonable searches and seizures and a state's interest in obtaining evidence through warrantless searches?

8. A court is considering a case of first impression. The court must decide whether it should adopt no-fault divorces. No-fault divorce allows couples to obtain a divorce by citing ir-

reconcilable differences, without proving fault. What are policy concerns the court should consider?

9. The court is considering the following case of first impression: The defendant was charged with assault and battery. The prosecution subpoenaed the defendant's wife to testify against him. The defense counsel argued that the wife should not be forced to testify against her husband.

What policy considerations should the court consider?

10. A statute requires convicted sex offenders to register with the police after their release from prison. The courts have held that convicted sex offenders are only required to register in the town where they reside. A court has articulated that protection of minors in the community outweighs the privacy interests of the ex-convicts. In a case now pending before the court, the District Attorney seeks to require convicted sex offenders to register in a county-wide registry.

Draft a policy argument on behalf of the District Attorney.

Chapter 6

Other Considerations

Objectives

WHEN YOU FINISH READING THIS CHAPTER AND COMPLETE THE
EXERCISES YOU WILL BE ABLE TO:

- DEFINE JUDICIAL CONSERVATISM;
- DEFINE FAIRNESS;
- INCORPORATE CONSERVATISM AND FAIRNESS IN LEGAL ARGU-
MENTS.

In addition to concepts discussed in previous chapters, legal
analysis may require the examination of several other considerations. This chapter explores judicial conservatism and fairness.
These concepts ensure a comprehensive analysis. Whether these
considerations impact your legal analysis depends on a variety of
factors, such as: the facts of your case, the legal issues, and the
law. Understanding that legal analysis may require several different considerations helps prevent an overly simplistic approach to
the analysis of legal problems.

A. Judicial Conservatism

Generally, courts are conservative. While courts may change
the law, they are reluctant to do so. One reason is because courts
are bound to follow precedent, pursuant to the doctrine of *stare
decisis*. Following precedent results in predictability. Deciding like

cases similarly also results in fairness. If courts constantly changed the law, society could not gauge the legal consequence of their actions.

No court likes to have its decision reversed. This contributes to the courts' conservative nature. Appellate courts can review lower courts' decisions when errors are alleged or when lower courts allegedly violate *stare decisis*. Consequently, some courts are reluctant to render legally risky rulings that push the limits of the law.

Although courts are conservative, the law does change. While courts do change the law and overrule precedent, it is rare. When change is appropriate, courts are cautious to maintain a logical evolution of the law. This caution causes some areas of the law to change quite slowly.

Judicial conservatism deters some courts from expressly overruling prior opinions. Instead, they express disapproval of an opinion by not endorsing a prior court's holding. Here, they may merely express disagreement or criticism with the prior court's opinion, without expressly overruling it. Out of respect to that court, the disapproval is often subtly stated.

Understanding judicial conservatism helps lawyers craft persuasive legal arguments. Lawyers formulate arguments that appeal to this disposition. Use the court's inherent conservatism to your benefit by arguing that your position fits squarely within the existing law. The court will be more receptive to this type of argument, because it will not have to make new law or even expand existing law.

Suppose a law allows employers to geographically restrict where their former employees can work. Employers, however, may only restrict former employees within reasonable geographic boundaries. Courts have consistently ruled that two-mile restrictions are reasonable. Your client, an employer, wants to hold one of its employees to a 1.8 mile restrictive covenant. The only question is whether this covenant is reasonable.

Your client could successfully argue that her covenant is reasonable. The 1.8 mile restriction is less than the two-mile restriction that courts have previously ruled are reasonable. The client's argument will most likely prevail because her argument falls squarely within the existing law. The court will not have to expand the law.

If your position requires the court to change the law, attorneys should try to persuade the court that the change is only a small extension of the existing law. An extension of the law, after all, is still a modification or change of the law. Courts are hesitant to modify established rules, but could be persuaded if the change of law is characterized as only a slight extension.

Referring to the above example regarding restrictive covenants, suppose your client seeks to restrict her employees to a 2.4 mile geographic restriction. Your client could argue that this distance is reasonable. Your client may persuade the court that her position is only a slight expansion of the two-mile geographic restriction allowed in prior cases. She should prevail because this slight extension of existing law is compatible with the court's conservative nature.

Courts, however, recognize a difference between slightly extending the law and starting down a "slippery slope" by opening up the floodgates to litigation. A slippery slope is a court's decision that expands the law without articulating a clear limit. Courts do not like to change the law, especially when that change could result in endless lawsuits clogging the court system. Perhaps Justice Grimes said it best when he criticized the majority opinion for starting down a slippery slope. He warned that the court "let the genie out of the bottle, and it would be impossible to stuff it back in." *Corso v. Merrill*, 406 A.2d 300, 309 (N.H. 1979) (Grimes, J., dissenting).

Consider a state law that allows people to recover for emotional distress when they witness a defendant injure a close family relation. Suppose a court considered whether a cousin could recover under this rule. The court may reason that if it allowed a cousin to recover, a slippery slope may result. If a cousin can recover, could best friends recover, what about a fiancé? Where would the court draw the line? To avoid a slippery slope, the

court may strictly construe the law, allowing only close family re-
lations to recover. On the other hand, if the court did not narrowly construe the law, it could allow a cousin to recover by
slightly extending the definition of a close family relation. As the
above example illustrates, there is a fine line between a slight extension of the law and teetering on the brink of a slippery slope.

B. Fairness

Fairness is the discretion of the court to consider the concepts
of equity, impartiality, and justness when resolving disputes.
While courts are bound to follow precedent, they do have discretion to consider fairness when following precedent would lead to
a fundamentally unfair result. Fairness considerations may also
influence a court if the law is unclear or unsettled. A thorough
analysis of legal issues should include fairness.

When making arguments, attorneys invoke sympathy for their
clients in order to appeal to a court's sense of fairness. Attorneys
remind courts that their cases affect real people, in real life situations. Fairness arguments, however, should be subtle. Melodra-
matic arguments will weaken a lawyer's credibility with a court.

A sound legal foundation combined with fairness considerations make a stronger argument than an argument based on fairness alone. Relying exclusively on fairness, without arguing the
merits of the law, might appeal to the court's innate sense of justice, but will not give the court a legal basis to rule in your favor.
Fairness should be used to bolster a legal argument, not replace it.

After providing a solid legal foundation, attorneys may remind
the court of the competing fairness interests of both parties in a
case. That argument would stress that a decision adverse to their
client would be disproportionately unfair compared to the effect
on their opponent. While attorneys have wide latitude when
making fairness arguments, they should all focus on the impact
of a court's decision on their clients.

Suppose the defendant built a garage that encroached five inches onto the property of his neighbor, the plaintiff. The plaintiff intends to sell her property, but cannot because of this encroachment. She asks the court to order the defendant to tear down his garage. The whole garage would have to be destroyed and built again on the defendant's land. The defendant can emphasize fairness, by arguing that tearing down his garage would be disproportionately unfair compared to the effect on the plaintiff. The defendant could ask the court to reach an outcome that would be fair to both parties, such as compensating the plaintiff for the encroachment.

Reminding the court of fairness implications may assist the court in reaching a decision that favors your client. While courts are bound to follow precedent, fairness considerations can still influence courts' decisions. Fairness could tip the scales of justice in your client's favor.

Practice Exercises

Consider the following exercises to reinforce your understanding of this chapter:

1. Define judicial conservatism.

2. Define fairness.

3. Name one reason why courts generally are conservative.

4. When drafting an argument that requires the court to expand the law, how can attorneys appeal to a court's conservative nature?

5. What does it mean when a court starts down a "slippery slope"?

6. Why is an argument based both on law and fairness stronger than an argument based on fairness alone?

7. Why is it important to be subtle when making a fairness argument?

8. A law legalized the use of marijuana for medicinal purposes. Courts interpreting this law have consistently ruled that it applies only to victims of terminal illnesses. A plaintiff has glaucoma, a non-fatal illness. The plaintiff seeks to use marijuana for medicinal purposes.

   Aware of the court's conservative nature, draft an argument that opposes an extension of the law.

9. Seller had a valid contract to deliver 100 widgets to Buyer's factory by 9:00 a.m. on January 8th. Due to severe traffic, on January 8, Seller arrived at Buyer's plant with the widgets at 9:22 a.m. Buyer refused to accept the widgets, because Seller was late.

   Draft a fairness argument that supports Seller's position.

10. Ryan and Isabelle dated for two years before deciding to buy a house together. They equally contributed their own

funds to purchase a house. Isabelle spent a lot of time carefully decorating and renovating the house. She bought all the furniture for the house with her own money. A year later, Ryan and Isabelle broke up. Ryan and Isabelle both want the house. Each wants the other person to move out. The court must now resolve the issue.

Draft a fairness argument to present to the court on behalf of Isabelle.

Chapter 7

The Legal Argument

OBJECTIVES

WHEN YOU FINISH READING THIS CHAPTER AND COMPLETE THE
EXERCISES PROVIDED, YOU WILL BE ABLE TO:

- UNDERSTAND THE ROLE AND FUNCTION OF ORGANIZATIONAL
  FORMULAS IN LEGAL WRITING;
- ORGANIZE A LEGAL ARGUMENT USING CREAC.

After understanding the analysis of a legal issue, lawyers focus
on the organization of the legal argument. Legal documents, such
as office memorandum or persuasive briefs, are the conduit for
the written communication of legal analysis. Through these documents lawyers present legal arguments in an organized, logical,
and clear manner.

A. CREAC

Lawyers typically draft two types of legal arguments: objective
and persuasive. An objective argument is unbiased and seeks to
educate the reader about the legal issue, and predict the likely legal
outcome of an issue. A persuasive argument is biased and seeks to
persuade the reader about the legitimacy of the legal argument.

Lawyers present these arguments in a number of formats. The
objective argument is often written in an interoffice memorandum. An interoffice memorandum is an internal document that

objectively summarizes the attorney's research and analysis, and predicts an outcome. The persuasive argument is generally written in a memorandum of law, or brief. A memorandum of law, or brief, is a persuasive document attorneys submit to a court in support of their client's legal position.

Many attorneys employ organizational formulas to clearly communicate their arguments. Students also use formulas or paradigms as a guide when drafting legal arguments. These formulas include, but are not limited to: **IRAC**, **CREAC**, and **CRAC**. In each of these formulas, each letter represents a specific component of a legal argument. For example, the letters in **IRAC** represent: Issue, Rules, Application, and Conclusion. Although several variations exist, all formulas are functionally similar.

Relying too heavily on formulas or paradigms, however, may weaken the argument. Often, students focus on formula rather than cogent analysis of legal problems. Students need to remember that these formulas are important organizational tools, but should never replace careful legal analysis.

This chapter will explain one paradigmatic formula, **CREAC**, and its function in legal writing. One benefit of the **CREAC** format is that it requires an explanation of the law before an application of the law to your client's case. **CREAC** has five component parts, each building on the latter. Each letter in **CREAC** represents a specific component of a legal argument: Conclusion, Rules, Explanation of the law, Application of the Law, and Conclusion. Each part, when combined, results in a cohesive, logical, and comprehensive argument.

CREAC Format	
C	Conclusion
R	Rules
E	Explanation of the Law
A	Application of the Law
C	Conclusion

This chapter will discuss an argument following the **CREAC** organizational format. The following example used to illustrate **CREAC** considers whether your client is liable for trespass. This argument will exemplify objective, or predictive, writing.

Your Client's Legal Problem

Your client, the Defendant, was sued for trespass. She suffers from seizures. While driving on a street that bordered Owner's land, your client had a seizure and lost control of her car. The car careened onto Owner's land, destroying his prized rose bushes.

The C in CREAC

Employing **CREAC**, organize the analysis of your client's legal problem. First, state your ultimate Conclusion regarding the particular issue discussed. This statement should be drafted in affirmative, precise language. If possible, include a brief summary of the reasoning that supports the conclusion. The **CREAC** formula requires a conclusion at the beginning of the argument because lawyers and courts are busy and expect to see the bottom line. Readers can better understand your analysis when they know the ultimate conclusion.

The "C" In Your Client's Case

The Court will likely rule that the Defendant did not trespass on Owner's land because she unintentionally entered Owner's land.

The R in CREAC

Next, state the Rule(s) governing the issue. As discussed in Chapter 2, rules can be derived from case law or enacted law, such as statutes. Keep in mind that there may be many rules applicable to the legal issue analyzed. State the general rule, if applicable, that governs the issue discussed. A general rule is the comprehensive legal principle that is relevant to the particular issue analyzed. Then, state more specific rules that address the issue discussed within the general rule. State the rules in order of increasing level of specificity.

Rules govern the outcome of the analysis and frame the organization of the analysis. As such, **CREAC** requires lawyers to identify rules at the beginning of the argument. Much like a game of poker, you cannot play the game if you do not understand the rules.

The "R" In Your Client's Case

Trespass to land prohibits the physical invasion of an unauthorized person onto another's real property. (*General rule*). An intention to trespass is not required, only an intention to enter the land. (*Specific rule*).[1]

The E in CREAC

Next, Explain the relevant authority interpreting or applying the rules. This section of **CREAC** consists of a holistic discussion that educates the reader about the law. An explanation of the law provides guidance for the reader by explaining how prior courts have resolved the same or similar issues. This section is particularly important in court briefs. In briefs, lawyers attempt to persuade a court that their explanation of the issues control. Therefore, it aids the persuasive value of their analysis. Pursuant to *stare decisis*, courts are bound to follow binding precedent. Reminding the court about the binding precedent in this section helps persuade the court to rule in your client's favor.

The explanation of the law section should include a discussion of the critical facts in cases, the courts' holding, and most importantly, the courts' reasoning. Consider including policy, fairness, and other considerations that the courts have addressed. Ultimately, this section should thoroughly educate the reader about the issues addressed in your legal problem.

The "E" In Your Client's Case

The court has determined what satisfies the element of intent for a trespass. In *Case B,* the court

---

1. Citations omitted throughout this example.

found that the defendant entered the plaintiff's property when he cut across an empty field. The defendant thought he was on public property. The court held that the defendant was liable for a trespass. The court ruled that an intent to enter the land of another, not an intent to commit a trespass, satisfies the prima facie tort of trespass. The court reasoned that although he did not intend to commit a trespass, he did intend to do the act which resulted in a trespass.

The A in CREAC

After explaining the law, Apply the law to the facts of your case. Employing the strategies discussed throughout this book, explain how the precedent relates to your client's case. If the facts of the precedent and your client's case are closely analogous or distinguishable, consider employing narrow analysis. If the facts of the precedent and your client's case are not readily comparable, but the reasoning of the precedent is applicable to your case, then consider employing broad analysis. Consider including policy and fairness arguments. Also, bear in mind the court's conservative nature when drafting arguments. Finally, consider including the opponent's arguments, if only to refute them.

The application section of **CREAC** is the most important component of the formula. This book has focused on the "**A**" in **CREAC**. The persuasiveness of this section will likely determine the outcome of the issue. Each component part of **CREAC**, however, is critical to communicating a well-reasoned and thorough argument.

The "A" In Your Client's Case

The Defendant will argue that *Case B* is distinguishable from the present case. Unlike the defendant in *Case B*, who intended to enter the Owner's property, the Defendant in the present case involuntarily entered Owner's land. The Court will most likely follow the reasoning of *Case B,* and similarly rule that the intent to do the act that resulted in the trespass, and not the act of trespassing, is required for trespass. The Defendant suffered a seizure, an involuntary physical act. As a result, she lost control of her car and inadvertently entered Owner' land. The Court will likely hold her not liable, because she never intended the act that resulted in the trespass.

The Plaintiff, however, will argue that *Case B* is analogous to the present case. Like the defendant in *Case B,* who intended to enter the Owner's property, the Defendant in the present case also intended to enter Owner's property. Following the court's reasoning in *Case B,* the Plaintiff will argue that the Defendant intended to drive her car knowing she suffered from seizures, therefore she intended the act that resulted in a trespass. The Plaintiff will contend that the Court will likely hold the Defendant liable.

The C in CREAC

The Conclusion should concisely state the legal outcome. This section should be brief and should never introduce new ideas. It reminds the reader of the bottom line.

The "C" In Your Client's Case

The Defendant will most likely prevail, because she did not intend the act that resulted in the trespass. The Court will not be persuaded by the Plaintiff's argument, because the Defendant's entrance onto Owner's land was caused by a seizure, an involuntary act. The Court will hold that the Defendant is not liable for trespass.

The CREAC Argument

Below, review your client's entire argument following the **CREAC** format. Notice how each component of **CREAC** builds upon the former. When combined, the entire argument should represent a holistic legal thought.

C   The Court will likely rule that the Defendant did not trespass on Owner's land because she unintentionally entered Owner's land. Trespass to land prohibits the physical invasion of an unauthorized person

R   onto another's real property. An intention to trespass is not required, only an intention to enter the land. The only issue raised in the Plaintiff's complaint is whether the Defendant intentionally entered the Owner's land.

    The court has determined what satisfies the element of intent for a trespass. In *Case B,* the court found that the defendant entered the plaintiff's prop-

E   erty when he cut across an empty field. The defendant thought he was on public property. The court held that the defendant was liable for a trespass. The court ruled that an intent to enter the land of another, not an intent to commit a trespass, satisfies the prima facie tort of trespass. The court reasoned that although he did not intend to commit a trespass, he did intend to do the act which resulted in a trespass.

    The Defendant will argue that *Case B* is distinguishable from the present case. Unlike the defendant in *Case B,* who intended to enter the Owner's property, the Defendant in the present case involuntarily

A   entered Owner's land. The Court will most likely follow the reasoning of *Case B,* and similarly rule that the intent to do the act that resulted in the trespass, and not the act of trespassing, is required for trespass. The Defendant suffered a seizure, an involuntary physical act. As a result, she lost control of her car and inadvertently entered Owner's land. The Court will likely hold her not liable, because she never intended the act that resulted in the trespass.

    The Plaintiff, however, will argue that *Case B* is analogous to the present case. Like the defendant in *Case B,* who intended to enter the Owner's property, the Defendant in the present case also intended to enter Owner's property. Following the court's reasoning in *Case B*, the Plaintiff will argue that the Defendant intended to drive her car knowing she suffered from seizures, therefore she intended the act that resulted in a trespass. The Plaintiff will contend that the Court will likely hold the Defendant liable.

    The Defendant will most likely prevail, because she did not intend the act that resulted in the trespass.

C The Court will not be persuaded by the Plaintiff's argument, because the Defendant's entrance onto Owner's land was caused by a seizure, an involuntary act. The Court will hold that the Defendant is not liable for trespass.

Review the Appendices for additional examples of both objective and persuasive writing using the **CREAC** format. Although lawyers recognize the danger of relying too heavily on organizational formulas, like **CREAC**, they can be quite useful for first-year law students. **CREAC** organizes the analysis of a legal argument.

B. Fourteen Tips When Drafting CREAC

    This book has focused on legal analysis, the "A" in **CREAC**. When using an organizational guide to legal arguments, keep the following fourteen points in mind. These points address traps that often ensnare law students.

Fourteen Tips for CREAC
1. Don't Be Conclusory.
2. Compare Fact to Fact.
3. Weave the Analysis.
4. Start With the Analogy.
5. Prove the Analogy.
6. Explain the Law Before Applying the Law.

7. Understand the Law Before Applying the Law.
8. Analyze One Issue at a Time.
9. Analyze the Opponent's Argument.
10. Don't Fight the Law.
11. Avoid the Stretch Argument.
12. Be Concise.
13. Remember the Alternative Argument.
14. Organize the Analysis Around a Common Thread

1. Don't Be Conclusory

Instead of merely stating the conclusion, explain how you reached that conclusion. Sometimes, after immersing themselves in a legal problem, students lose perspective and assume that the reader is already acquainted with the law and analysis. To avoid this, explain each step of the analysis. Don't assume the reader will understand your argument without a clear, logical analysis of the issue. Like giving someone directions to your house, explain each small step so your reader won't get lost.

> **Ineffective:** I live at 55 Mt. Auburn Street. Drive to exit four, then turn left. At the light, turn left onto Mt. Auburn Street.

> **Effective:** I live at 55 Mt. Auburn Street. After entering Interstate Highway 88 West, drive for six miles. Turn off at exit four, and bear left onto Storrow Road. At the first light, make a left turn onto Mt. Auburn Street. The third house on the left, a three-story brick colonial, is my house.

2. Compare Fact to Fact

Whenever possible, refer to a critical fact in the precedent when comparing that fact to a fact in your client's case. Don't merely mention the precedent without showing which facts in the precedent are comparable to the facts in your client's case. Don't make the reader refer back to an explanation of a case to see how the facts in that case apply to your client's case. Lay it out for the reader. The reader should never have to "work" to follow your analysis.

Ineffective: Like the defendant in *Jones*, our client also has an alibi because he was home during the alleged crime.

Effective: Like the defendant in *Jones*, who had an alibi because he was in a movie theater during that alleged crime, our client also has an alibi because he was at home during the alleged crime.

3. Weave the Analysis

Don't layer the analysis by repeating the explanation of a precedent, followed by a list of facts from your client's case, without showing how one relates to the other. Instead, weave the law and facts together. Refer to the fact in the precedent and then compare that fact to your client's case. Show the reader the connection or relationship between the cases.

Ineffective: In *Jones*, the defendant proved his alibi by showing evidence that he was in a movie theater during the alleged crime. The *Jones* court held that the defendant was not guilty. The court reasoned that a defendant who establishes an alibi cannot be found guilty of a crime. In this case, our client was home at the time of the crime. Therefore, he has an alibi.

Effective: Both the *Jones* defendant and our client have alibis. Like the defendant in *Jones*, who had an alibi because he was in a movie theater during that alleged crime, our client also has an alibi because he was home during the alleged crime.

4. Start With the Analogy

At the outset of the analysis, compare the precedent to your client's case. Do not start the analysis by listing facts in your client's case. State the comparison between the precedent and your client's case and then support it or prove it by referring to facts in your client's case.

Ineffective: Our client was home at the time of the alleged crime.

Effective: Both the *Jones* defendant and our client have alibis. Like the defendant in *Jones*, who proved that he had an alibi because he was in a movie theater during that alleged crime, our client also has an alibi because he was at home during the alleged crime.

5. Prove the Analogy

After stating an analogy or distinction, prove the legal assertion using the reasoning of the precedent. Tell the reader why your comparison is significant.

Ineffective: Both the *Jones* defendant and our client have alibis. Like the defendant in *Jones*, who proved that he had an alibi because he was in a movie theater during that alleged crime, our client also has an alibi because he was home during the alleged crime. Therefore, our client is not guilty.

Effective: Both the *Jones* defendant and our client have alibis. Like the defendant in *Jones*, who proved that he had an alibi because he was in a movie theater during that alleged crime, our client also has an alibi because he was home during the alleged crime. This Court should follow the reasoning of *Jones*, that defendants who establish sufficient evidence of an alibi cannot be found guilty of the crime. This Court should hold that the Defendant is not guilty because he establishes sufficient evidence of an alibi.

6. Explain the Law Before Applying the Law

Before applying a case to the facts of your case, make sure you previously explained it. Then, you can refer to that case when applying it to your client's case. Discussing a case for the first time within the analysis is confusing to the reader. The reader then has to comprehend the facts, holding, and reasoning of that case, as well as understand how it compares to your client's case.

Ineffective: In *Jones*, the court concluded that the defendant was not guilty of robbery. The defendant in

Jones was at a movie theater during the alleged crime. The court held that defendant had an alibi during the crime. The *Jones* court reasoned that defendants who establish sufficient evidence of an alibi cannot be found guilty of the crime.

The *Smith* case is distinguishable to the present case. Unlike the defendant in *Smith* who alleged that he had an alibi, but failed to prove it, the Defendant in the present case presented witnesses who established his alibi. Moreover, both the *Jones* defendant and our client have alibis. Like the defendant in *Jones*, who proved that he had an alibi because he was in a movie theater during that alleged crime, our client also has an alibi because he was at home during the alleged crime. This Court should follow the reasoning of *Jones* that defendants who establish sufficient evidence of an alibi cannot be found guilty of the crime. This Court should hold that the Defendant is not guilty because he establishes sufficient evidence of an alibi.

Effective: Several courts have determined the sufficiency of an alibi. For example, the court in *Smith* held that the defendant was guilty because he did not have an alibi during the alleged crime. The defendant claimed that he was at a restaurant, but could not substantiate this claim. The *Smith* court reasoned that without sufficient evidence to support his alibi, it must fail.

In *Jones* the court concluded that the defendant was not guilty of robbery. The defendant in *Jones* was at a movie theater during the alleged crime. The court held that the defendant proved that he had an alibi during the crime. The *Jones* court reasoned that defendants who establish sufficient evidence of an alibi cannot be found guilty of the crime.

While the *Smith* case is distinguishable to the present case, the *Jones* case is analogous. Unlike the defendant in *Smith* who alleged that he had an alibi, but failed to prove it, the Defendant in the present case presented witnesses who established his alibi. Moreover, both the *Jones* defendant and our client have alibis. Like the defendant in *Jones*, who proved that he had an alibi because he was in a movie theater during that alleged crime, our client also has an alibi because he was at home during the alleged crime. This Court should follow the reasoning of *Jones* that defendants who establish sufficient evidence of an alibi cannot be found guilty of the crime. This Court should hold that the Defendant is not guilty because he establishes sufficient evidence of an alibi.

7. Understand the Law Before Applying the Law

Make sure you thoroughly understand the law before you attempt to apply it to your client's case. You can't analyze the law until you understand it. Your analysis will reflect any confusion regarding the law. A confusing analysis will frustrate the reader and defeat its purpose.

8. Analyze One Issue at a Time

Analyze a single legal issue at a time. Do not analyze several issues at once. Smaller bites are easier to swallow.

9. Analyze the Opponent's Argument

Don't ignore the opposing argument. Ignoring it won't make it go away. Predict the other side's likely argument and incorporate those arguments into your analysis.

Ineffective: While the *Smith* case is distinguishable to the present case, the *Jones* case is analogous. Unlike the defendant in *Smith* who alleged that he had an alibi, but failed to prove it, the Defendant in the present case presented witnesses who established his alibi. Moreover, both the *Jones* defendant and our client have alibis. Like the defendant in *Jones*, who proved that he had an alibi because he was in a movie theater during that alleged crime, our client also has an alibi because he was at home during the alleged crime. This Court should follow the reasoning of *Jones* that defendants who establish sufficient evidence of an alibi cannot be found guilty of the crime. This Court should hold that the Defendant is not guilty because he establishes sufficient evidence of an alibi.

Effective: While the *Smith* case is distinguishable to the present case, the *Jones* case is analogous. Unlike the defendant in *Smith* who alleged that he had an alibi, but failed to prove it, the Defendant in the present case presented witnesses who established his alibi. Moreover, both the *Jones* defendant and our client have alibis. Like the defendant in *Jones*, who proved that he had an alibi because he was in a movie theater during that alleged crime, our client also has an alibi because he was at home during the alleged crime. This Court should follow the reasoning of *Jones* that defendants who establish sufficient evidence of an alibi cannot be found guilty of the crime.

The prosecution will argue that *Jones* is not applicable. The alibi witnesses in *Jones* were reliable. In contrast, in this case they are biased. The prosecution's argument is unpersuasive because the reliability of a witness is a question of fact for a jury to decide. This Court should hold that the Defendant is not guilty because he establishes sufficient evidence of an alibi.

10. Don't Fight the Law

It is unethical to omit unfavorable authority or bend the law so it fits within your intended conclusion. Instead, deal with the law head-on. Try to distinguish authority that is negative to your legal position.

11. Avoid the Stretch Argument

Legally tenuous or far-fetched arguments will likely fail and undermine your credibility with the court. Careful, logical analysis is usually more persuasive than an "all or nothing" long shot.

12. Be Concise

Make your point and move on. Avoid repetition and confusing legal jargon. Courts and lawyers are busy and value brevity.

13. Remember the Alternative Argument

Cover all your bases. An alternative argument should be thoroughly addressed and analyzed. Try to provide the court with several options to rule in your favor.

14. Organize the Analysis Around a Common Thread

When a large body of case law is applicable to your issue, organize your analysis around the common thread derived from the precedents, instead of analyzing each case separately.

Practice Exercises

Consider the following exercises to reinforce your understanding of this chapter:

1. What is the purpose of **CREAC**?

2. What is the danger of relying too heavily on organizational formulas?

3. Complete the following questions:
   a. What do the letters of **CREAC** represent?
   b. What is the purpose of the **E**?
   c. What is the purpose of the **A**?

4. Why is it important to state the conclusion first in an argument?

5. The following sentences are from an argument. Unscramble the sentences and put them in a logical order following **CREAC**.
   a. Voluntary manslaughter is the unlawful killing of another without malice, but with adequate provocation. Utopia Gen. Law § 52 (1997).
   b. Like the defendant in *State v. Z*, who was adequately provoked when he found his wife in bed with another, the defendant in the present case was also adequately provoked when he was cut off by a speeding motorist on a crowded highway. In the heat of passion, with no time to reflect on the consequences of his actions, the Defendant in the present case, like the defendant in *State v. Z*, committed voluntary manslaughter. In the present case, the Defendant, after being cut off by a speeding motorists, pulled a hand gun from his glove compartment, and shot the speeding driver.
   c. The Defendant in the present case is guilty of voluntary manslaughter because he killed another in the heat of passion.

d. The present court should follow the reasoning of the court in *State v. Z*, where the court reasoned that killings that result from adequate provocation, or in the heat of passion, are voluntary manslaughters. The court will find that the Defendant committed voluntary manslaughter.

e. In *State v. Z*, the defendant found his wife in bed with another. Consumed with rage, the defendant grabbed a shotgun and killed the victim. The court in *State v. Z* held that the defendant was guilty of voluntary manslaughter because he killed another in the heat of passion. The court in *State v. Z* reasoned that the defendant committed voluntary manslaughter because he was reasonably provoked and reacted without time to reflect on his actions.

6. Review the arguments in appendices A and B. In the margin, see if you can identify each **CREAC** component in those arguments.

Conclusion

Legal analysis is a skill, unique to the legal profession. Sophisticated legal analysis is the result of careful thinking, critical reading, and experience. Mastering legal analysis is attainable by understanding the basic principles discussed in this book. By providing an introduction and foundation to legal analysis, we hope this book helps you understand *legal analysis—the fundamental skill.*

Appendix A

Interoffice Memorandum

Although this book focuses on legal analysis, not specifically on legal writing, it is helpful to see the type of legal documents that incorporate legal analysis. Lawyers communicate legal analysis in many types of documents. The two most common conduits of analysis are the court brief and the interoffice memorandum. Both are considered memoranda of law. The interoffice memo is an **objective** document for internal-office use only. In contrast, the court brief is a **persuasive** document submitted to a court.

An interoffice memorandum is one type of an objective legal document. Typically, supervising attorneys ask associates to research a legal issue and draft an internal memorandum of law summarizing their research, analysis, and prediction of the outcome(s). An interoffice memo serves two important purposes. First, it educates the reader about the law relevant to a legal issue. Second, it predicts how a court will likely decide a legal issue. An interoffice memo honestly assesses the strengths and weaknesses of a client's legal position. Read the example below to see how lawyers incorporate legal analysis in an interoffice memorandum.

Romantz & Vinson
41 Oak Street, Suite 402
West Natick, MA 01760
(508)-655-2231

INTEROFFICE MEMORANDUM OF LAW

TO: Senior Partner

FROM: Associate

DATE: March 18, 1991

RE: *Hall v. Hall*: The Doctrine of Interspousal Immunity

I. FACTS

Brenda Hall ("Plaintiff") is suing our client, Stuart Hall ("Defendant"), for libel, an intentional tort. The Plaintiff seeks damages for written statements the Defendant published that allegedly injured her reputation and exposed her to public contempt and ridicule. The Defendant seeks to bar the action, relying on the doctrine of interspousal immunity.

The Plaintiff and Defendant were married on June 15, 1967, in Gloucester, Massachusetts. At the time of their marriage, the Plaintiff was a computer consultant with Biotech, Inc. ("Biotech"), located in Warren, Massachusetts. The Defendant was a software manager with that same company. Over the ensuing twenty-four years, both parties remained at Biotech. The Defendant rose to the position of Senior Manager, while the Plaintiff was able to secure an executive-level position, and a seat on the Board of Directors.

In March of 1991, the Plaintiff was nominated by the Board of Directors to assume the position of Chief Executive Officer for Biotech. The CEO is responsible for the day-to-day operations of the company and receives a yearly bonus which includes both stock options and salary enhancements. The Board of Directors decided to vote on the Plaintiff's candidacy in September of 1991.

On June 11, 1991, the Defendant published an article in "The Techie," Biotech's bi-monthly newsletter. In that article, the Defendant accused the Plaintiff of "employing clever accounting techniques" and "bilking the company out of millions of dollars." The article also claimed that the Plaintiff never graduated from college.

In September of 1991, the Board of Directors voted to remove the Plaintiff from office and placed her on a temporary suspension pending an investigation of the allegations made in the article. Two weeks later, Biotech fired the Plaintiff. In October of 1991, the Plaintiff separated from the Defendant. Neither party has filed formal dissolution or separation documents with the court. This memorandum analyzes whether the doctrine of interspousal immunity bars the Plaintiff's lawsuit.

II. QUESTION PRESENTED

Under Massachusetts case law, does the doctrine of interspousal immunity bar an· action brought by a spouse, commenced after she separated from her spouse, for libel committed during the marriage?

III. BRIEF ANSWER

Yes. The doctrine of interspousal immunity will bar an action in tort between spouses when a court has not judicially severed the marriage. The court will allow law suits between spouses if they neither breach the privileged aspects of marriage, nor disrupt the peace and harmony of the marital home. The court, however, has restricted the application of interspousal immunity for some actions in tort between spouses. The court will not bar suits between spouses when the injury results from an automobile accident. In the present case, the Plaintiff filed suit against the Defendant, her husband, for libel that allegedly occurred during the marriage and neither have moved to legally terminate the marital relationship. The court will bar this action because the injury did not result from an automobile accident, and the suit would disrupt the peace and harmony of the marriage.

IV. APPLICABLE LAW

Case law derived from the courts of the Commonwealth of Massachusetts will determine the outcome of this matter.

V. DISCUSSION

The court will most likely bar the Plaintiff's action for libel because the doctrine of interspousal immunity prohibits suits between married parties. The doctrine of interspousal immunity bars causes of action between spouses for a tort committed during marriage. *Callow v. Thomas*, 78 N.E.2d 637, 638 (Mass. 1948). Recently, the court has limited its application. *Noguiera v. Noguiera*, 444 N.E.2d 940 (Mass. 1982); *Brown v. Brown*, 409 N.E.2d 717 (Mass. 1980); *Lewis v. Lewis*, 351 N.E.2d 526 (Mass. 1976). Interspousal immunity no longer bars a cause of action between spouses for injuries sustained in an automobile accident. *Lewis*, 351 N.E.2d at 532. The doctrine also has no application to suits between spouses after an entry of a divorce *nisi*. *Noguiera*, 444 N.E.2d at 940.

The courts of the Commonwealth originally adopted the common-law rule of interspousal immunity for three reasons. *See Callow*, 78 N.E.2d at 638; *see also Lewis*, 351 N.E.2d at 527-29. First, the doctrine prevents the conceptual problem of the single marriage entity suing itself. *Lewis*, 351 N.E.2d at 527; *Callow*, 78 N.E.2d at 638. Second, it supports the fundamental institution of marriage. *Callow*, 78 N.E.2d at 638. Allowing a cause of action in tort between spouses would disrupt the peace and harmony of a family. *Lewis*, 351 N.E.2d at 529. Third, the doctrine prevents a husband and wife from reaping fraudulent and collusive rewards at the expense of liability insurers. *Id.*

In *Callow v. Thomas*, the court first considered whether it should abolish the doctrine of interspousal immunity. *Callow*, 78 N.E.2d at 638. In *Callow*, the husband injured his wife in a car accident when he drove into a tree. *Id.* at 637. Soon thereafter, the wife petitioned the court to annul the marriage. *Id.* Two months after the court declared the marriage null and void, the wife commenced an action in tort to recover for her injuries. *Id.*

at 638. The *Callow* court held that the doctrine of interspousal immunity bars actions in tort between spouses that arise during the marriage despite the later dissolution or nullity of the marriage. *Id.* at 641. The court reasoned that events during the period of the putative marriage should not be re-visited after a later annulment. *Id.* The court concluded that the existence of a marital relationship barred the action even after a declaration of annulment. *Id.*

Later, in *Lewis v. Lewis,* the court reconsidered the doctrine of interspousal immunity. *Lewis,* 351 N.E.2d at 526. In *Lewis,* the wife sustained injuries when her husband struck a light pole with his car. *Id.* at 527. The court allowed the lawsuit to proceed, carving out an exception to the doctrine of interspousal immunity for injuries arising only out of automobile accidents. *Id.* at 532. The *Lewis* court noted that plaintiffs who suffer tortious injury should recover unless there is strong public policy to bar recovery. *Id.* While the *Lewis* court intimated that the policy behind interspousal immunity protects the peace and harmony of the marital relationship, it questioned whether this immunity guards against family discord. *Id.* at 529. The court reasoned that the policies supporting the doctrine of interspousal immunity were inadequate when considered against the facts of the case before it. *Id.* at 532. The *Lewis* court limited its holding to only suits that arise out of automobile accidents. *Id.* at 532-33. While concluding that claims arising out of automobile accidents were no longer barred, the court expressly refused to abolish the doctrine completely. *Id.* Instead, the court implicitly preferred a case-by-case inquiry that weighed both policy considerations that support immunity and any inequities that may result. *Id.*

In *Brown v. Brown,* the court was asked to extend its holding in *Lewis* and considered whether the doctrine of interspousal immunity bars suits between spouses for personal injuries not arising out of automobile accidents. *Brown,* 409 N.E.2d at 717. In *Brown,* the wife sustained injuries when she fell on property her husband owned and maintained. *Id.* The court noted the trend toward the judicial abrogation of the doctrine and the antiquated assumptions that supported it. *Id.* The court concluded that the doctrine should not bar an action between spouses for personal injury unless that action would disrupt "the privileged or consensual aspects of marriage." *Brown,* 409 N.E.2d at 717. Remanding the case to the trial court for reconsideration, the court directed the lower court to determine whether the tortious behavior in the case did disrupt the privileged and consensual aspects of marriage. *Id.* at 719. As in *Lewis,* the *Brown* court declined to abolish the rule. *Id.* Instead the court opted to determine immunity on a case-by-case basis. *Id.*

In *Noguiera v. Noguiera,* the court was again asked to consider the continued vitality of the doctrine of interspousal immunity when it was raised to bar actions for intentional torts between spouses committed after an entry of a divorce *nisi. Noguiera,* 444 N.E.2d at 940. The court also determined when the "privileged or consensual aspects of marriage" require interspousal immunity. *Id.* at 941. In *Nogueira,* the husband instituted a suit for libel and intentional infliction of emotional distress. *Id.* His wife wrote to her husband's National Guard superior alleging that he had a drinking problem, psychological problems, and attempted to smother her with a pillow. *Id.* The wife wrote the letter four days after a court granted an order that provisionally severed the marital relationship, or a divorce *nisi. Id.*

The *Nogueira* court held that the interspousal immunity doctrine did not bar suits for intentional torts committed after a marriage is severed by a divorce *nisi. Id.* The court reasoned that tortious behavior that occurs after the provisional severance of a marriage "does not affect the privileged or consensual aspects of married life." *Id.* The court noted that only strong public policy arguments can justify the judicially created immunity. *Id.* at 942, *quoting Lewis,* 351 N.E.2d at 532. Chief among these arguments is the belief that tort actions between spouses would disrupt the peace and harmony of the marital home. *Nogueira,* 444 N.E.2d at 942. The court reasoned that the marriage in the present case was nothing more than "a shell" at the time of the alleged tort. *Id.* The court declined to find any marital harmony that would require interspousal immunity, despite the fact that a judgment of divorce *nisi* does not permanently sever the marriage. *Id.* Impliedly, however, the court ruled that tort actions between spouses that would disrupt the peace and harmony or "privileged or consensual aspects" of the marital family would require invocation of interspousal immunity. *Id.*

In the present case, the Defendant will argue that *Nogueira* is distinguishable from the present case. Unlike the *Nogueira* marriage, which was legally severed by a divorce *nisi* at the time of the tort, in the present case the alleged tort occurred during the marriage and the spouses have only informally separated. The Defendant will remind the court of the *Nogueira* opinion, which ruled that interspousal immunity will bar actions in tort, but not when the marital relationship is judicially severed. The Defendant will distinguish the divorce *nisi*, a judicial severance of the *Nogueira* marriage, to the mutual, non-judicial, separation in the present case. He will argue that while a divorce *nisi* ripens into a final divorce decree, a mutual separation of marital partners may result in reconciliation. Therefore, the reasons behind interspousal immunity, which preserve the peace and harmony of marriage and protect the consensual aspects of the marital relationship, do apply in the present case.

The Defendant will also argue that while courts have recently reconsidered the absolute bar to actions in tort between spouses, the court has only limited the application of immunity to actions arising out of automobile accidents. If the court concludes that interspousal immunity bars the Plaintiff's action, a slippery slope could result. The *Noguiera* court only allowed a cause of action in personal injury between a husband and wife that did not arise out of an automobile accident, because that marital relationship was already judicially severed by a divorce *nisi* at the time of the tort. Therefore, the reasons underlying interspousal immunity no longer applied. Furthermore, while the *Brown* court implicitly allowed personal injury claims between spouses, it remanded the case to the trial court with instructions to consider whether the lawsuit would disrupt the "privileged or consensual aspects of married life." As such, that court implicitly directed the trial court to allow the action if the application of immunity would not protect the peace and harmony of the marital relationship. The Defendant will ask the court to enforce the interspousal immunity doctrine and bar the Plaintiff's cause of action, because the suit would disrupt the peace and harmony of their marriage.

The Plaintiff, however, will likely argue that *Nogueira* is applicable. Like the marriage in *Nogueira*, which was terminated by a divorce, the marriage in the present case was also terminated, but by a separation. The Plaintiff will point to the *Nogueira* opinion which ruled that interspousal immunity will not bar actions in tort when the marital relationship is already severed. The Plaintiff will liken the divorce in *Nogueira* to the mutual, albeit non-judicial, separation in the present case. She will argue that both a divorce and separation indicate that the marriage is over. Therefore, the reasons behind interspousal immunity, which preserve the peace and harmony of marriage, do not apply.

The Plaintiff will also argue that the court should not bar the present action, because the court has substantially limited, and continues to limit, the application of the antiquated doctrine of interspousal immunity. The Plaintiff will point to the *Lewis* court, which limited interspousal immunity for injuries sustained in automobile accidents; and the *Nogueira* court, which held that a claim of intentional tort between spouses was not barred by the doctrine. The Plaintiff will argue that the court should follow the trend toward the judicial abrogation of the interspousal immunity doctrine and the antiquated assumptions that support it. Moreover, the Plaintiff will argue that this court should follow the *Lewis* court's reasoning that plaintiffs who suffer tortious injuries should recover unless strong public policy supports a bar to recovery. She will argue that no policy exists in today's society to support a bar to her recovery. She will ask the court to continue limiting the inequitable application of the interspousal immunity doctrine by allowing her cause of action.

The court will likely rule in favor of the Defendant. While the court has limited the application of the doctrine of interspousal immunity, it has only done so when the claim arises out of an automobile accident or when the court has severed the marriage before immunity is claimed. The court will bar the present suit, because the cause of action is for an intentional tort, not an automobile injury, and the marriage has not been judicially severed.

VI. CONCLUSION

For the foregoing reasons, the court will likely bar the Plaintiff's action.

Appendix B

Persuasive Memorandum of Law

A persuasive brief is sometimes referred to as a memorandum of law. A persuasive brief is a formal legal document submitted to a court on behalf of a client. A persuasive brief is different from an objective memo for several reasons. First, the purpose of each memo is different. Unlike an objective interoffice memorandum, which educates the reader about the law and predicts the likely result of a legal issue, a persuasive brief argues that a court should adopt a client's legal position. Second, the audience for each memo is different. Supervising attorneys read objective memos. Judges, however, read persuasive briefs. Third, the tone of each memo differs. Objective memos are an unbiased, honest appraisal of your client's legal position. In contrast, persuasive memos are slanted to favor your client's position. The following example illustrates how attorneys incorporate legal analysis in a persuasive document.

FLORIDA CIRCUIT COURT
ORANGE COUNTY

****

STATE OF FLORIDA,   *

      Prosecution,   *   C. A. No. CR-96-1324

v.   *

MARY ANDERSON,   *

      Defendant.   *

****

STATE OF FLORIDA'S MEMORANDUM OF LAW
IN OPPOSITION
TO DEFENDANT'S MOTION TO DISMISS

The State of Florida ("State") requests that this honorable court deny Defendant Mary Anderson's ("Defendant") Motion to Dismiss. The State charged the Defendant with solicitation to commit murder in violation of Florida statutes chapter 777.04(2). Fla. Stat. ch. 777.04(2) (1997). Pursuant to Rule 3.190(c)(4) of the Florida Rules of Criminal Procedure, the Defendant has filed a motion to dismiss. This court should only grant the Defendant's Motion to Dismiss if the most favorable construction to the State does not establish a prima facie case of guilt. *State v. Duque,* 472 So.2d 758, 762 (Fla. Dist. Ct. App. 1985). Looking at the evidence in the light most favorable to the State, this court should deny the Defendant's Motion to Dismiss because the evidence supports a prima facie case that the Defendant solicited another to commit murder.

FACTS

The Defendant married her husband in June of 1967 in Milton, Texas. They relocated to Florida City, in August of 1976. The Defendant secured a position at a local television station, KRTV, and soon rose to the position of news-anchor for its popular evening news program.

In September of 1994, the Defendant began having an affair

with her assistant, James Clark ("Clark"). Clark began working at KRTV in the Fall of 1992, after graduating from Central Florida College. The couple often spent weekends together under the ruse of working on news-related stories. They were also seen together by colleagues and friends in Florida City throughout their relationship. The Defendant considered the relationship to be a casual affair, while Clark believed it was far more serious.

In November of 1996, Clark began to pressure the Defendant to divorce her husband. Citing professional reasons, the Defendant consistently refused Clark's demand. In December of that same year, the Defendant decided to end the affair with Clark. She sent him a short note indicating her intention to cease the affair and requested that he no longer contact her. Despite the Defendant's efforts, Clark continued to pursue her, sending flowers to her office, and calling her personal phone line between four and eight times a day. The Defendant ignored the phone calls.

Finally, on January 10, 1997, Clark called the Defendant at her office and threatened to expose their affair to her husband and the press. The Defendant understood the damage the news of the affair would have on her career and became extremely angry. She threatened to get even with Clark if he exposed the relationship.

The Defendant told her secretary, Sue Berg, to cancel the rest of her appointments that day. Then, for three hours, the Defendant sat in her office and considered Clark's threat. At 4:15 p.m., Berg informed the Defendant that Arthur Jackson was in the office and needed to speak with her right away about a news story. Arthur Jackson, an ex-convict and a useful confidential informant for KRTV, was an important source the Defendant had used for several stories. She agreed to see Jackson.

When Jackson entered the Defendant's office, he noticed she had been crying. He asked if there was anything he could do. The Defendant replied, "Yeah, if you know how to get rid of my problem." Jackson responded, "What do you mean, Mary?" She replied, "I need a permanent solution and quickly." "About what," asked Jackson. Just then, Clark entered the Defendant's office. The Defendant looked at Jackson and said, "about him." The Defendant ordered Clark out of her office. After Clark left the office, the Defendant turned to Jackson and said, "if he isn't stopped, he's sure to destroy me. He has information that can ruin me personally and professionally." Laughing, the Defendant said, "you owe me, now help me take care of this." Jackson then responded, "By this time tomorrow, the problem will have vanished." As Jackson left her office, the Defendant laughed, "if it was only that easy."

Facing an unrelated criminal charge, Jackson saw the Defendant's situation as an opportunity to negotiate a plea with the prosecutor. Jackson called the District Attorney's office and spoke to an assistant district attorney. Jackson told the attorney that he was just asked to kill someone and related the entire conversation with the Defendant. The police investigated and later arrested the Defendant. A grand jury later indicted the Defendant for solicitation to commit murder in violation of Florida statutes chapter 777.04(2).

The Defendant filed a Motion to Dismiss the indictment. Based on the foregoing facts, the court should deny the Defendant's Motion to Dismiss because the evidence proves a prima facie case that the Defendant solicited another to commit murder.

ARGUMENT

I. THE COURT SHOULD DENY THE DEFENDANT'S MOTION TO DISMISS BECAUSE SHE UNLAWFULLY SOLICITED ANOTHER TO COMMIT MURDER WHEN SHE ENCOURAGED AND REQUESTED JACKSON TO KILL CLARK INTENDING THAT HE DO SO.

The court should deny the Defendant's motion to dismiss because the evidence satisfies all the elements of solicitation. Pursuant to Florida statutes chapter 777.04(2), criminal solicitation requires that a defendant (1) encourage, command, hire, or request another to commit an offense, and (2) intend that the other commit the offense. *The Florida Bar v. Marable*, 645 So.2d 438,

442 (Fla. 1994). Under Florida case law interpreting the judicial standard for a motion to dismiss, the court should deny a motion to dismiss if intent is an issue, because criminal intent is a question of fact best left for a trier of fact. *State v. Gaines,* 431 So.2d 736, 737 (Fla. Dist. Ct. App. 1983). As such, this court should deny the motion to dismiss because intent is an element of criminal solicitation. Should the court consider intent, however, the evidence shows that the Defendant intended the solicitee to commit the crime. The Defendant also satisfied the other element of solicitation by encouraging Jackson to murder Clark. The court should deny the Defendant's motion to dismiss.

A. The Court Should Deny The Defendant's Motion To Dismiss Because Only The Trier Of Fact Should Determine Intent; But If The Court Does Consider Intent, It Should Conclude That The Defendant Satisfied The Intent Element Of Solicitation Because The Conversation Between The Defendant And Jackson Establish Criminal Solicitation.

The court should not consider the Defendant's intent in a motion to dismiss because intent is a question of fact for a trier of fact to decide. If the court considers intent, however, it should conclude that the Defendant intended Jackson to kill Clark. One element of solicitation requires a defendant to intend the person solicited commit a crime. *Marable,* 645 So.2d at 442. Only the trier of fact should determine a defendant's intent after observing all the witnesses. *Gaines,* 431 So.2d at 737. The court should deny the Defendant's motion to dismiss because it should not consider the Defendant's intent. Even if the court considers intent, the evidence establishes that the Defendant did intend that Jackson kill Clark.

1. The Court Should Not Consider The Defendant's Intent In A Motion To Dismiss, Because Only A Trier of Fact Should Decide Intent After Observing All Of The Witnesses.

The court should not consider intent in the Defendant's motion to dismiss. Whether a defendant intended an act is a question for a trier of fact. *Gaines,* 431 So.2d at 737. While the court may consider a defendant's intent on a motion when the evidence clearly establishes intent or the lack thereof, this is the exception, and not the rule. *Id.* The trier of fact may infer intent from a defendant's acts and the circumstances. *Id.*; *Marable*, 645 So.2d at 443.

In *State v. Gaines*, the court considered the intent of the defendant in a motion to dismiss because the question of intent was clear from the record. *Gaines*, 431 So.2d at 736. The *Gaines* court reviewed transcripts of taped conversations between the defendant and the solicitee, an undercover detective. *Id.* at 737. The court determined that the defendant's intent was without question and clearly established from the evidence, and thus was a matter of law, not fact. *Id.* at 738. The *Gaines* court did not deny the motion, despite the question of intent, because that intent was clear from the record. *Id.*

In a subsequent case, the court criticized the *Gaines* opinion, by reaffirming that intent is a question for the trier of fact. *State v. Waskin*, 481 So.2d. 492, 498 n.3 (Fla. Dist. Ct. App. 1985). The *Waskin* court noted that the issue of the defendant's intent to have the crime committed is for the jury to resolve after examining all the evidence. *Id.* Denying the motion to dismiss, the court expressed its disbelief that a taped conversation could only have one interpretation because sometimes words cannot be taken at face value. *Id.* at 498 n.3, 499.

The court should not consider the Defendant's intent in this motion to dismiss. Like *Waskin*, where the court denied a motion to dismiss because intent was an issue, this court should deny the motion because intent is also an issue. The *Waskin* court reasoned that a trier of fact, not a court considering a motion to dismiss, is uniquely qualified to determine questions of intent. The court should apply the reasoning of *Waskin* by having the jury resolve the question of the Defendant's intent after the jury has had the opportunity to review all of the evidence and the testimony of the witnesses.

The Defendant's intent is not clear and thus the court should not decide her intent in this motion to dismiss. Unlike the facts in *Gaines,* where the lack of intent was clear, and thus established that the defendant lacked intent as a matter of law, the conversation between the Defendant in the present case and Jackson does not clearly show, as a matter of law, that the Defendant lacked intent. While the *Gaines* court reviewed recorded conversations, this court only has written statements. The Defendant will rely on *Gaines* and argue that both cases demonstrate clear evidence of intent. Thus, the court should consider the motion. This argument is unpersuasive because the court should not resolve the issue of the Defendant's intent when the evidence does not clearly show, as a matter of law, the Defendant's intent.

> 2. If The Court Decides To Consider The Defendant's Intent, Then It Should Conclude That The Defendant Satisfied The Intent Element Of Solicitation Because Her Words And Circumstances Demonstrate That She Intended That Jackson Kill Clark.

If the court decides to consider the Defendant's intent, it should conclude that the Defendant did intend that Jackson kill Clark. One element of solicitation requires a defendant to intend that the person solicited commit the crime. *Marable,* 645 So.2d at 442. The court may infer intent from the defendant's words of request or the circumstances of the solicitation itself. *Id.* at 443. Circumstantial evidence may be the sole evidence of a defendant's mental state. *Id.* In a motion to dismiss, however, the court must resolve all inferences taken from the evidence against the defendant. *Duque,* 472 So.2d at 762.

The Florida courts have determined what satisfies the intent element of solicitation. In *Florida Bar v. Marable,* the Florida court of Appeals held that the defendant did not solicit another to commit a crime because although his words could be construed as encouragement or a request, he lacked the requisite intent. *Marable,* 645 So.2d at 443. The defendant in *Marable,* an attorney, allegedly committed the criminal offense of solicitation for burglary when he informed his client of the location of incriminating photographs and told him "you can break in there and steal them." *Marable,* 645 So.2d at 441 The defendant testified that he was not serious when he made the comment about the theft to his client. *Id.* at 441. Moreover, the court found that the defendant told the solicitee that he was not serious. *Id.* Based on the defendant's testimony and his explanation of the circumstances surrounding the alleged solicitation, the *Marable* court held that the defendant was not serious, therefore did not intend for the solicitee to commit the crime. *Id.* at 443.

In *Gaines*, the court granted the defendant's motion to dismiss because the defendant lacked the necessary intent. *Gaines,* 431 So. 2d at 736. While the defendant in *Gaines* discussed maiming her stepson, the court concluded that she would decide at a later date if she wanted the hitman to commit the crime. *Id.* at 737-38. The *Gaines* court reasoned that the defendant had reached the threshold of committing the solicitation, but did not cross it. *Id.* at 736. That defendant considered whether the crime should occur, not when it should occur. *Id.*

The Defendant in the present case did have the requisite intent for solicitation. Unlike the defendant in *Marable*, who was not serious about soliciting a crime and therefore could not intend the crime, the Defendant in the present case was not kidding. The *Marable* court, after examining the defendant's testimony and his explanation of the circumstances of the alleged crime, found no criminal intent because he told the solicitee that he was kidding about the crime. In contrast, the Defendant in the present case was serious because she stated to Jackson that he owed her and he should help her take care of her problem. Moreover, Jackson responded that the problem would be gone by the next day, indicating that he took her statements seriously. The actual words the Defendant used, as well as the circumstances surrounding her conversation with Jackson, show that she intended for Jackson to kill Clark.

The Defendant will argue that like the defendant in *Marable*, who was not serious and therefore did not intend the solicitation, she was also only kidding during the conversation with Jackson. She will point to the fact that she laughed on two separate occasions during her conversation with Jackson. This argument is not persuasive because while the defendant in *Marable* expressly stated that he was only kidding about the alleged solicitation, the Defendant made no such statements, instead she encouraged Jackson to kill her former lover. For the purposes of this motion to dismiss, this court must resolve any inferences against the Defendant. *Duque*, 472 So.2d at 762. Therefore, this court should conclude that the Defendant had the requisite intent for solicitation.

B. The Court Should Deny The Defendant's Motion To Dismiss Because The Defendant Satisfied The Encouragement Element Of Solicitation When She Directed Jackson To Murder Clark.

The Defendant satisfied the second element of solicitation because she encouraged Jackson to murder Clark when she communicated her desire for Jackson to kill Clark. This element of solicitation requires a defendant to command, hire, request, or encourage another person to commit a crime. Fla. Stat. ch. 774.04(2) (1997). The person solicited to commit the crime need not actually commit the crime nor intend to commit the crime. *Brown v. State*, 550 So.2d 142, 143 (Fla. Dist. Ct. App. 1989); *State v. Johnson*, 561 So.2d 1321, 1322 (Fla. Dist. Ct. App. 1990). The type of conduct which may constitute encouraging does not require an overt or affirmative act. *Duque*, 472 So.2d at 762. They key word in the statute is "encourage." *Id.* Nor does solicitation require that a defendant perform a specific act, set a specific time for the crime to occur, or pay the solicitee. *Waskin*, 481 So.2d at 497-98. The gist of the first element of criminal solicitation is enticement. *Hutchinson v. State*, 315 So.2d 546, 548 (Fla. Dist. Ct. App. 1975).

The Florida legislature enacted the law against criminal solicitation to protect society from the harm that would result if a solicitee committed a crime, and to prevent solicitor's from inviting or enticing members of society to commit a crime. *Waskin*, 481 So.2d at 493-94. In *State v. Duque*, the Florida District Court of Appeals denied the defendant's motion to dismiss, concluding that the a trier of fact could determine that the defendant's acts encouraged another to commit a crime. *Duque*, 472 So.2d at 762. In *Duque*, the defendant repeatedly told others that her family would be better off if her ex-husband was dead, noting that she would receive a large life insurance policy upon his death. *Id.* at 760-61. The court reasoned that even though she did not participate in the planning of the murder, there is no limit as to the type of conduct that may constitute encouragement. *Id.* at 762. The court further noted that criminal solicitation does not require an affirmative overt act. *Id.*

Similarly, in *Waskin*, the court denied a defendant's motion to dismiss because a reasonable fact-finder could conclude that the defendant's conduct constituted encouragement or a request of another to commit murder. *Waskin*, 482 So.2d at 498-99. The defendant in *Waskin* met with an undercover officer, who the defendant believed was a hitman, to discuss the killing of his ex-wife. *Id.* at 492-97. The undercover officer taped a conversation in which the defendant told the officer that his "problem" was his ex-wife, and he needed something "permanent" done. *Id.* at 494. Although they did not come to a final agreement, the defendant told the officer he would give him his ex-wife's address, her licence plate number, and picture. *Id.* at 495-97. They also agreed to meet again for further discussions. *Id.*

The *Waskin* court held that sufficient evidence existed for a jury to determine that at the very least the defendant had requested or encouraged, if not actually hired, the officer to kill his ex-wife. *Id.* at 498. The court held that even though neither the time of performance nor method of payment was finalized, the Defendant still committed solicitation. *Id.* at 498. The *Waskin* court reasoned that a clear request for another to commit a crime is sufficient to establish the encouragement element of solicitation. *Id.*

The Defendant in the present case encouraged another to commit a crime. Like the defendant in *Duque*, who made statements regarding how her life would be better if her ex-husband was dead, the Defendant in the present case told Jackson that Clark would destroy her if he was not stopped. Similar to the defendant in *Duque*, whose conduct was sufficient for a jury to conclude that she encouraged another to commit a crime, the Defendant's conduct in the present case also encouraged another to commit a crime. This court should follow the *Duque* court's reasoning that there is no limit regarding the type of conduct that may satisfy the encouragement element of solicitation.

Similarly, like the defendant in *Waskin*, who clearly requested that another kill his ex-wife, the Defendant's comments in the present case also clearly request another to kill her ex-lover. Parallel to the defendant in *Waskin* who stated that his ex-wife was his "problem" and he needed a "permanent" solution, the Defendant in the present case told Jackson that Clark was her "problem" and that she also needed a "permanent" solution. This court should follow the *Waskin* court which reasoned that a clear request to commit a crime, despite no specificity as to payment or time, satisfied the encouragement element of solicitation. In this case, even though the Defendant and Jackson never agreed as to the specific time or financial arrangements for the murder, the Defendant's clear request is sufficient to show encouragement.

The Defendant will argue that unlike the defendant in *Waskin,* who clearly requested another to commit a crime, she did not clearly request that Jackson kill Clark. She will point to the fact that she never expressly asked Clark to kill anyone. This argument is unpersuasive, however, because the Defendant's words, actions, and circumstances are sufficient for a reasonable factfinder to conclude that the Defendant encouraged Jackson to kill Clark. The court should deny the Defendant's motion to dismiss because the Defendant committed solicitation when he encouraged Dawson to commit murder.

CONCLUSION

For the reasons stated herein, the court should deny the Defendant's Motion to Dismiss.

Respectfully submitted,
STATE OF FLORIDA
By its Attorney,

_____

Ima Lawyer BBO#12345
Law & Law, P.C.
41 Day Street
Flagler Beach, FL 32136
(919) 555-1212

Dated: March 11, 1996.

CERTIFICATE OF SERVICE

I, Ima Lawyer, certify that I caused a true copy of the State of Florida's Memorandum of Law in Opposition to the Defendant's Motion to Dismiss to be mailed, first class, postage pre-paid, to counsel for the Defendant, Attorney Rollins.

Dated: March 11, 1996

Appendix C

Client Letter

Another document lawyers draft that incorporates legal analysis of issues is called a client letter. A client letter is loosely defined as any communication between an attorney and client, or the attorney and another party on behalf of the client, regarding a legal issue. Among other purposes, they usually (i) respond to a client's legal question, (ii) offer a formal opinion on a client's legal issue, (iii) or demand another party do something on behalf of your client's legal interests. Client letters typically lack both the formality of a court brief, and the detail of an interoffice memorandum because the audience is the client or other lay person, and not another attorney or a judge. The tone and tenor of the client letter should consider the audience's legal sophistication, or lack of it.

Law Offices of J.P. Teacher

1145 North Main Street
Somece, PA 11223
Office (213) 555-0090
Fax (213)555-5435
jpteacher@law.com

June 1, 1998

Mr. Howard Colbert
One Holmer Avenue
Smith, PA 98777
(555) 555-1234

      Re: **Colbert v. Grant; Libel**

Dear Mr. Colbert:

On our meeting on May 17, 1998, you asked us whether you have a cause of action for libel against your supervisor, Lisa Grant, when she wrote a letter which characterized your lifestyle as "immoral" that later resulted in your termination from the Smith Public School District. As discussed more fully below, we conclude that you do have a cause of action against Grant for the tort of libel.

Our analysis is premised on the following facts, as you reported them to me on May 17, 1998. You served as Director of Food Services for Smith Regional High School until August of 1996. In August of that same year, Lisa Grant, the assistant principal for Smith Regional High School and your immediate supervisor, discovered that you are gay. Ms. Grant later informed the school superintendent of her discovery. They both decided that you should be fired. Ms. Grant then informed you, in writing, that due to budget cuts, your contract would not be renewed for the 1996-97 academic year. This letter was forwarded to the Smith School Committee together with an addendum written by Ms. Grant which stated that your "immoral lifestyle" prevented the school from renewing your contract. This letter was marked "confidential." Per local ordinance, this letter and addendum was read into the public record and later published in the Smith Gazette, a local newspaper.

Based on my research, Grant's letter of termination with the attached addendum is libelous. Under Pennsylvania law, libel is any maliciously written or printed material that tends to damage the reputation of another. While the original termination letter was not libelous, that letter with the attached addendum was libelous.

A cause of action for libel consists of five elements: 1) whether a remark is capable of defamatory meaning; 2) whether the defendant published a remark; 3) whether the remark applies to the plaintiff; 4) whether the audience understands the remark as the defendant intended; and (5) whether harm resulted from the remark. Written or printed remarks made in the employer/employee context, however, are not actionable for libel even if they satisfy the five-part libel test.

The first element of libel, whether a remark is capable of defamatory meaning, is satisfied because Grant's characterization of your lifestyle as "immoral" in the addendum she attached to the termination letter is defamatory. Any communication that damages a person's standing in the community is defamatory. Grant's statement was defamatory because it can damage your standing in the community. Moreover, Grant cannot take advantage of the employer/employee libel defense because her remarks related to your lifestyle and not your work performance.

The second element, whether the defendant published a remark, is also satisfied because Grant's letter was read by third parties. In order to satisfy the publication element of libel, a remark must be communicated to a third person. Grant published the libelous remark because her letter was read into the public record at the school committee meeting and the letter was published in the Smith Gazette, a local newspaper. Therefore, the remark was communicated to a third person.

The third and fourth elements are also met. The third element, whether the remark applies to the plaintiff, is satisfied because the libelous remarks did apply to you. Ms. Grant expressly named you in her letter to the school committee.

The fourth element of libel, whether the audience understands the remark as the defendant intended, is satisfied because the audience understood the defamatory nature of the letter as Grant intended. The context in which the defamatory letter is written and the audience are both considered when determining whether this element is satisfied. In this case, it is reasonable to infer that the audience understood the term "immoral lifestyle" as Grant intended.

Finally, the fifth element, whether harm resulted from the remark, is satisfied because Grant's letter did harm you. Here, only likely harm is required, not proof of an actual harm. The damaging impact of Grant's letter will likely prevent you from securing employment in any school district in the area. As such, the letter will harm you.

Under the circumstances outlined above, and as you reported them to me on May 17, 1998, we conclude that you have a cause of action against Lisa Grant for libel. If any of the facts as described above are inaccurate, please call this office as soon as possible so that we can re-evaluate your claim.

I hope this letter has been helpful to you. There is a time limit to file this type of action. Therefore, please call this office by August 17, 1998, so we may discuss your next course of action.

Very truly yours,

J.P. Teacher, Esq.

Glossary of Terms

Analogical analysis. A strategy of legal analysis that employs analogies by comparing facts in cases or the characteristic of facts in cases.

Analogy. An inference that if two or more facts or characteristics are similar in one respect, they will be similar in other respects.

Appellate court. A court that reviews errors of law made in a prior court's determination of the same case.

Attorney. A person admitted in a jurisdiction to practice law.

Authority. Any legal source used by courts and attorneys to oppose or support a legal proposition.

Balancing test. A test that consists of several factors that courts weigh to reach a conclusion.

Bill. A draft of a proposed law introduced by a legislator.

Binding Authority. Law that a court must follow.

Broad analogy. An analogy that draws general fact comparisons that relate to, but are not necessarily parallel to, the critical facts of the precedent.

Case. A judicial proceeding that determines a controversy between two or more parties.

Case-at-bar. A cause of action currently before a court.

Case law. Law derived from the judiciary.

Case of first impression. A case that raises an issue not yet resolved by the court, and thus, no precedent exists.

Case synthesis. A process that combines several opinions in order to identify a common denominator among the precedents.

Certification. A procedure authorized by state law that refers a state issue originally brought in federal court to that state's highest court of appeals.

Common law. The rules and legal principles derived from judicial decisions, judgments, and decrees, in the absence of enacted law.

Concurring opinion. A separate opinion that agrees with the result of the majority opinion, but for different reasons.

Court. A branch of government that interprets the law and resolves legal disputes.

Court brief. A persuasive memorandum of law that attorneys submit to a court in support of their client's legal position. (Do not confuse this with students' case briefs).

CRAC. An organizational formula for legal writing that represents: Conclusion, Rule(s), Application of the law, and Conclusion.

CREAC. An organizational formula for legal writing that represents: Conclusion, Rule(s), Explanation of the law, Application of the law, and Conclusion.

Critical facts. Facts from the controlling precedent that a court found dispositive when it resolved a legal dispute.

Decision. The judicial determination of a dispute.

Dictum (dicta). The part of a court's opinion that does not relate to the resolution of the case.

Disposition. The component of an opinion that resolves a legal matter.

Dissenting opinion. A separate opinion that disagrees with the majority's opinion.

Distinction. A contrast between the critical facts of a precedent and the facts in a case-at-bar.

Ejusdem generis. ("Of the same kind.") A maxim of statutory construction that requires courts to construe a general word in a statute, that follows a list of specific words, to include only things of the same type specified in the list.

Element. A component part of a test that must be satisfied or met.

Enacted law. Law derived from a legislature.

Extrapolation. A process of identifying a common characteristic among several facts, by abstracting more general characteristics from specific traits.

Factor. A component part of a test that the court considers. Every factor need not weigh in favor of a party to satisfy a test.

Facts. The events, circumstances, or objects stated in an opinion that relate to the ultimate resolution of the matter.

Fairness. A court's considerations of equity, impartiality, and justness, when deciding legal issues.

Hierarchy. Different levels of courts within a jurisdiction.

Highest court of appeal. The highest level appellate court within a jurisdiction.

Holding. (Held) The component of an opinion that resolves the question(s) presented to the court.

In pari materia. ("On like subject matter.") A maxim of statutory construction that requires courts to read statutes on the same subject matter consistently with each other and requires courts to construe provisions of the same statute consistently.

Intermediate court of appeals. An appellate court that reviews errors of law from a trial court in jurisdictions that have a three-level court hierarchy.

Interoffice memorandum. An internal legal document that summarizes an attorney's research and analysis. It objectively predicts a court's decision regarding specific legal issues.

Instrumentality. A means to achieve an end.

IRAC. An organizational formula for legal writing, that represents: **Issue**, **Rule**(s), **Application** of the law, and **Conclusion**.

Issue. The component of an opinion that presents the legal question that the court is asked to resolve.

Judge. A person who presides over legal disputes and decides controversies between parties.

Judgment. A court's final determination of a dispute that resolves the rights and liabilities of parties in a lawsuit.

Judicial conservatism. A court's inherent reluctance to change the law.

Jurisdiction. The power of a court to decide a case or controversy.

Law. Rules which govern society's conduct.

Lawyer. A person licensed to practice law.

Legal analysis. Strategies lawyers employ to determine, predict, or persuade legal outcomes of cases.

Legal test. A judicial inquiry that determines whether a rule has been satisfied.

Legislative history. The paper trail of a bill as it works its way through the different stages of the legislative process.

Legislative intent. The reasons behind the enactment of a law.

Legislature. The branch of government that enacts laws.

Maxim. An established principle of law.

Memorandum of law. A document summarizing a lawyer's research and analysis.

Narrow analogy. An analogy that draws specific fact comparisons between the case-at-bar and the precedent.

"On point." A case that is dispositive of the legal issue in your client's case.

Opinion. Written statement of a court explaining how it reached its decision.

Persuasive authority. Law that a court is not bound to follow, such as a case from another jurisdiction.

Persuasive brief. A formal written document submitted to a court to convince it to resolve an issue in a particular way.

Plain meaning doctrine. The rule of statutory construction that requires courts to interpret the meaning of a word or phrase in an unambiguous statute as it is generally accepted by reasonable persons.

Point sentence. A topic sentence that introduces the point of an analysis.

Policy. The purpose behind a law. The reason why a legislature or courts made a law. It considers how the law impacts society.

Precedent. A judicial decision or opinion that serves as an example of how a subsequent court can resolve a similar question of law under a similar set of facts.

Prima facie case. A case that alleges sufficient evidence on its face.

Primary authority. A source of authority that represents the law.

Procedural history. The component of an opinion that traces the case as it worked its way through the court system.

Prong. A component part of a test that may be either an element or a factor.

Prong test. An inquiry that requires the consideration of several parts in order to satisfy a test.

Reasoning. The component of an opinion that explains how the court reached its decision.

Rule. A principle of law employed or adopted to resolve a legal issue. A legal principle set by an authoritative body prohibiting or requiring action or forbearance.

Rule synthesis. A process that blends relevant cases to develop a holistic rule that incorporates the holdings of the applicable cases.

Secondary authority. A source of authority that consists of any relevant source, other than the law. It is persuasive, never binding, on a court.

Slippery slope. A judicial determination that results in unclear limits of liability, increasing the amount of lawsuits.

Stare decisis. ("Those things which have been so often adjudged ought to rest in peace.") A principle that requires courts to follow precedent when deciding similar cases.

Statute. An act of a legislature that, among other things, proscribes and governs conduct. It is a formal written enactment of a legislature.

Statutory analysis. A two-step process of legal analysis that requires courts and lawyers to construe statutes and analyze case law to determine the meaning and application of a statute.

Statutory construction. A judicial process that interprets statutes.

Totality of the circumstances test. A test that requires the court to consider all of the circumstances relevant to the case, instead of one factor or element.

Trial court. A court where evidence is first introduced and considered.

Index